Branding & AI

Branding & AI

Leveraging Technology to Generate Brand Revenue

Chahat Aggarwal

BEP

BUSINESS EXPERT PRESS

Leader in applied, concise business books

Branding & AI: Leveraging Technology to Generate Brand Revenue

Cover design by Charlene Kronstedt

Interior design by Exeter Premedia Services Private Ltd., Chennai, India

First published in 2021 by
Business Expert Press, LLC
222 East 46th Street, New York, NY 10017
www.businessexpertpress.com

ISBN-13: 978-1-63742-080-5 (paperback)
ISBN-13: 978-1-63742-081-2 (e-book)

Business Expert Press Marketing Collection

Collection ISSN: 2169-3978 (print)
Collection ISSN: 2169-3986 (electronic)

First edition: 2021

10 9 8 7 6 5 4 3 2 1

To my little brother Akshay,
my parents, and in loving memory of Eddy.

Description

The book discusses the intrinsic value of what branding is and the vital role that artificial intelligence (AI) can play in businesses' present and future success. The necessity to create noteworthy strategies and maintain consistency in the growth of brands is credited to adapting to the dynamic market deeply influenced by ever-growing technology. Brand awareness is a significant element in the success of businesses in highly competitive and saturated environments. It describes how branding on an organizational and personal level is directly proportional to profit and return on investment, along with how one can measure it. To elaborate, case studies of successful and unsuccessful marketing strategies of big brands have been dissected to showcase the impact of brand perception. The book further transgresses into the role of AI in branding, which can help companies achieve their highest goals through targeted marketing with the help of unbiased information gathered by machine intelligence. It also points out the limitations of AI and the factors to note while relying on machine versus human capabilities. The future of AI appears to be evidently intertwined with marketing initiatives, and the sectors most likely to be impacted have been described in detail.

The book can be used as a tool to translate corporate missions into execution with an innovative strategy for positive results.

Keywords

marketing strategy; case studies; branding and marketing; artificial intelligence tools; increase revenue; business growth and principles; amazon case study; worksheet and templates; tone of voice; brand personality; mission and vision

Contents

Review Quotes

"This is a very informative and well guided breakdown of how to brand your business. Explained in an easy-to-follow, practicable fashion, this is not your ordinary business book. This is the book that gives you actual pathways to generate revenue for your business."—**Ela Martin, CEO, Rebell Studios, Poland**

"This book is the game changer; it gives you the practical know-how of implementing the right strategy for your business. With case studies for both successful and unsuccessful marketing for big brands it gives extremely useful resources and implementation plans."—**Robert D, Global Creative Consultant, London**

"Want a book that explains how branding and AI can grow your business? This is IT. The author does a great job of keeping the contents easy to understand, up-to-date with the latest developments, and giving away the list of AI tools and marketing case studies, all of this while keeping the readers sane and engaged."—**Vikas Uberoy, Cybersecurity Channel Director, ANZ, Australia**

"If you want to create a brand like Coca-Cola, Amazon, Starbucks, Apple but don't know how or have money to hire a professional? This book is the answer to all your brand, business and A.I. queries to make your company rise to the top!"—**Jaynish Vaghela, Data Scientist, University of Texas, USA**

Welcome to the world of brand and artificial intelligence, the future of building efficient revenue

Preface

From the first footstep that marked humankind's beginning to this day and hour, when we are racing to the never-ending yet ever-present destination of absolute progress and development, we never stopped doing one thing; evolving. If Darwin talked about evolution in terms of physical changes to adapt to the changing environment, today, that growth is in terms of intellect. The fruit of that evolution is visible in the field of technology, where the magic of the human brain is wielded to ease our journey to the pedestal of development, the epitome of progress, hypothetically speaking.

Humans change. However, some traits remain the same. Just like love, poetry, music, and dance that aged like fine wine and whose glory is still untouched by the ravages of time, so are the human desires and longings to be the best, to have the best. If not for that desire, we would still be out there, hunting and gathering. Our ancestors' curiosity mingled with an eye for the best is what fueled this journey. Today, what baffles the human quest for the best is not the lack of choices but the abundance of the same. Everyday people, "the potential customers" face an avalanche of brands and products, all equally eye-catching and glossy. Prada, Dolce, Coca-Cola, McDonalds, Gucci, and the list goes on.

However, the few names mentioned attract the eye faster than the rest. There is a reason why they are the first in the never-ending and ever-growing list. Why, despite the clichéd generation gap, Prada and Gucci mean the same to a 50-year-old grown-up and a 14-year-old who is growing up. The key to this is a simple word with a noble suit of armor, branding. Just like Ptolemy and Antigonus was to Alexander the Great, so is branding to a business. If the former helped expand the kingdom, the latter helps develop the business and leave the so-called and much sought after "mark." The mark keeps the brand on the topmost shelf of the customers' minds with a shiny glow that never fails his notice. The "mark" that marks the product as the best.

In elementary words, branding is the key that opens the world of opportunities for a business. To put it better, *"branding distinguishes a product from the terms, highlighting its unique features and leaving an identifiable impression in the customers' minds."*

However, every mark needs to be painted with special ink to maintain an invaluable spot. An ink that is an equal blend of uniqueness and innovation splashed with intelligence and logic. And, branding is no different. For a brand to stand out, it needs a well-drawn out and thorough strategy with a pinch of magic. And, this magic is that extra bit of brain cell, which we have to use to brace up our brand to stand the test of time and, in the present context, the aggressive competition that springs like mushrooms during monsoon.

To get a firm footing in such a competitive environment, we need strategies that blend intellect and creativity. The same road is taken by the successful brands that have left a permanent mark.

And today, with technological advancements and progress, it's all about prudently employing that technology to make a difference. That's where artificial intelligence is added to branding—an epic blend with the legendary outcome.

Acknowledgments

First, I would like to thank my colleagues Nivedita, Sandra, and Vidhi who helped research this book and whose invaluable insights shape this beautiful study of brand and artificial intelligence. I must thank my mother, Anu Aggarwal, who constantly reminded me of the importance of quality writing and made sure I complete this book on time. Her insights on the structure of the book is what made such a complex topic—easy to explain. I would like to thank my family and friends who gave me very useful feedback on the readability and the engagement quotient from a reader's point of view and pushing me to do better.

—Chahat Aggarwal

Introduction to Branding and AI

To understand the role of artificial intelligence (AI) in branding, a thorough understanding of branding must be in place. It is more or less the take-off point of our knowledge and the firm base on which one can build.

The American Marketing Association defines a brand as

> A name, term, design, symbol, or any other feature that identifies one seller's goods or service as distinct from those of other sellers. The legal term for the brand is a trademark. A brand may identify one item, a family of items, or all items of that seller. If used for the firm as a whole, the preferred term is a trade name.

In simple words, the brand is the identity that creates a mark that keeps the firm or the product alive in the customers' minds. Amidst the torrent of choices, a lasting brand keeps up the product's glow in the customers' minds and, by default, creating a permanent space in the market from where it can expand and grow. However, the catch is about juxtaposing the term "lasting" with the brand. And, when looked through an unfiltered lens, it can seem like a Herculean task. However, with a strategy filter, it is clear that creating a lasting brand is all about prudent and wise planning blended with creativity and innovation. When working toward this end, the prime place should be given to the customer since; ultimately, it is a satisfied customer that rockets the brand to a place of success. That's where the how, when, and what of branding comes in.

How to satisfy the customer? What is the best strategy to make them stay? And the answer is straightforward yet complex, just like the Sphinx puzzle that Oedipus cracked with a tiny bit of sense. The customer visits when they feel special. When they are treated with a certain level of personal care adhering to their likes and dislikes, that's when they feel at home and home, as we know, is where people stay. The next focus is on personalized customer care, which is where AI makes its entry. It offers a peek into the future while having a firm footing on the present and a cautious eye toward the past.

To answer the "how" related to AI, some success stories of certain brands have made that mark and established themselves as unique and special.

The Amazing Journey of Amazon

As a firm, Amazon doesn't need any introduction. Every single human who has knocked on the door of online shopping and retail must indeed have met the king of retail whose throne has remained in the zenith of success for quite a long time. Despite the backbreaking competition, its position has remained atop, and it doesn't seem like the global leader in retail is going to step down any time soon. With its high net worth that just crossed 170 billion USD, Bezos and Amazon are moving forward with its unstoppable energy.

Every success will have a story behind it. The key. The reason and, in a more dramatic sense, the trade secret. And, what is Amazon's? Apart from excellent sales and great marketing strategies, what was the extra ingredient that accelerated its success? And, if it is not yet evident, it is nothing but the subtle art of employing AI that made all the difference. They tapped into the vast ocean of advancing technology and reaped the fruit. They call it "Flywheel." Their approach to AI fueled their growth and success and still keeps doing so. In engineering jargon, a flywheel is a simple tool that stores rotational energy when a machine is not working at a constant level. It saves the energy that is usually lost while switching on and off and spreads it to other parts of the machine.

And, the flywheel approach keeps the innovation on track by spreading the energy and knowledge from one area to another. It's a fine example of channeling the power from the matrix to specific parts, thereby powering up the whole. The innovation around machine learning in one area enhances the efforts of other teams, who employ this technology to fuel their products, thereby spreading the innovative streak throughout the organization. And, to add to this is Amazon was one among the pioneers who ventured into the then murky waters of AI, and inevitably, their courage to think out of the box paid off. And by default, it also enjoys the advantages that come with the territory of tapping into a field that experiences growth bursts day by day.

AI connects and maintains the balance between different parts of the firm. If the technical explanation is hard to comprehend, let us try to understand it through a very famous name. A name that has indeed become a household star and the most extraordinary proof that Amazon has managed to create its mark—Alexa. It was the most incredible machine learning stunt that was an absolute success. Alexa's integrations with Amazon Music, Prime, and personalized product recommendations round off this picture. Another essential role of AI is how it caters to the recommendation engine, the primary revenue source, which is a perfect example of how personalized customer experience powered by AI can take a brand to the topmost position.

What paved the way for their success was the timely and innovative use of AI and the willingness to take up the risk of trying out a technology that was still a half foot present and half foot future. We all know what happened later; the rest is history.

The Mile Hike of Nike

Who can be a stranger to the smooth "swoosh" and the ringing words "Just Do It." True to their essence, they just did it as well. Athletics is all about sportsman spirit and to rush forward with energy and confidence. And Nike, being one of the top brands that brought some of the finest and coolest sportswear, tapped into their spirit for novelty, and it made all the difference. With AI, they made sure that they have fitted shoes to top this competition to reach the top place in the market, and they did.

And, with their system that allows customers to design their sneakers in-store, Nike touches the finish line of personalized service. The trophy is visible in how Nike's name spills out during any conversation that lurks around sports. The cleverness quotient is also intact because the sneaker designing is more than just a stunt to impress the customers. It helps to collect a considerable amount of data that can be used by machine learning algorithms to design future apparel and to deliver personalized recommendations. Talk about pairing innovation with intelligence, and it's evident that Nike has bagged it. And, as it is apparent, AI has equipped the brand to face any race and retain its position without fail. And, the brand can shout with its head held high, "Just Do It."

Success Behind Starbucks

The aromatic cup of coffee with its mesmerizing flavors and old-school charm and "Starbucks" might have already crossed your mind. Starbucks uses its loyalty card and mobile app to collect customer data, which can be productively used to offer personalized customer service. Anyone will be happy to see recommendations made, especially according to their preferences while driving into a cafe, and that happiness is widely reflected in Starbucks' sales success. It uses predictive analytics to achieve this end, and also the virtual barista app powered by AI adds a perfect frame to this picture.

This prudent use of technology helped Starbucks keep up its pace and place with the avalanche of competition and come out unscratched and victorious. It is all about strategy and planning and a pinch of confidence to think out of the box, not very different from the courage one needs while switching from Frappuccino to Vanilla Latte. The courage that results in a happy experience, which makes the risk worth it.

Coca-Cola: The King of Soft Drinks Market

1.9 billion drinks, 500 brands, 200 countries. The daunting numbers aren't a matter of concern for Coca-Cola because it's fuel is sourced from the advancing domain of AI, which smoothens the rough patches and hard turns. It is with the help of AI that the company keeps a balance between the multitude of choices and the corresponding amount of data. They prudently use their vending machines fitted with AI algorithms that promote drinks and flavors most likely to be preferred in diverse locations. The company also uses AI in social media to analyze customer preferences and choices.

Suppose we talk about a company with a long-standing legacy, Coca-Cola. There would always be a curious question as to how the empire kept standing despite the advent of newer brands and challenging competition. The answer is as simple as it's tricky. They upgraded themselves with time and technology, keeping a sharp focus on the market's pulse and customers' preferences. Their road to success is smooth now because they put in efforts in the base labor, which is paying off now.

These are very few among the long list of success stories written by the ink of advancing technologies like AI, making a world of difference in branding and marketing. AI is no longer a nebulous domain filled with hazy mazes. It has evolved and is evolving into a promising technology that can rocket businesses to the top of the market.

CHAPTER 1

Overview

Branding 101 introduces the reader to the art and science of branding. A brand is more than just a logo that upholds the values and principles it caters to. The name and tagline is the brand's immediate face, the first sight element that projects the brand to the world. A brand becomes successful when it succeeds in arousing a certain level of attachment in the customer, making them return to the product despite the never-ending list of newer products and brands that sprout in the market like mushrooms in monsoon. The exploration of the idea of a brand helps in the evolution of the brand and branding process. The Theory of Brand Culture is further explained through its offers for an improved model of business branding. Defining strong brand values allows a brand's consumers to measure those values against their own. The fundamental elements include the brand compass, company culture, name and tagline, identity, voice and messaging, website, and brand architecture. Brand architecture is the coordinated system of names, colors, symbols, and visual language that defines a brand or brands. Maximizing authenticity with branding can open up the doors to every corner of the world, thereby becoming the most impactful and cost-effective way to deliver a holistic branding experience to the target audience.

Branding 101

Years ago, Aristotle's footnotes about Tragedy and Drama, most commonly known among the lovers of literature as "The Poetics," threw new light into understanding a genre intricately woven with many complexities. The most remarkable discovery that enhanced the knowledge was the central idea of "catharsis." However, ironic as it sounds, Aristotle never defined catharsis despite being the defining element of a Tragic play. And to this day, catharsis is a defining element without a proper definition.

So is a brand. Defining a brand can be quite a nebulous road because of the amalgamation of different concepts that build up one's understanding of the word. And one reason for this is that brand is not a mechanical aspect displayed into a linear set of terms and sentences or rather a consistent frame. **The brand is about perceptions, and perceptions differ from person to person, place to place.** A brand is the manifestation of the idea that humans are extraordinarily diverse and view everything through their customized filter of unique experiences and choices. And this innate personal element is the source of its growth potential. Despite technological advances and machines invading the realm of uncertainty, the fact remains that humans are emotional beings. Tapping into that source is the best way to capture their attention because when a business or a product can be free, the personal aspect is still light-years away.

IDENTITY
who you really are
+
IMAGE
who you people
think you are
BRAND

A brand is one of the company's most valuable assets. It represents the company's face, in the form of a recognizable name, logo, slogan, or an identifying symbol, mark, word, and/or sentence that companies use to distinguish their product from others. A combination of one or more of those elements can be utilized to create a brand identity. The brand is how a company is often referred to as, and they become the same. A company's brand carries a monetary value in the stock market (if the company is public), affecting stockholder value as it rises and falls. For these reasons, it's crucial to uphold the integrity of the brand.

Despite conducting research and analysis to deduce this idea into a simple definition, one will find oneself stuck in an unknown territory since customers themselves at times cannot pinpoint or underline a reason for their preference for a particular brand. And this lack of factual knowledge is not an empty space or void. Instead, it is a vast space with opportunities and scope, wherein you can build up newer and better territories and add in new layers to the understanding of the idea.

And when faced with this dilemma or when in need of a more fixed idea, it is best to cater to the argument put forth by Marty Neumeier, author and speaker who defines brand by laying out what a brand is not. *"A brand is not a logo. A brand is not an identity. A brand is not a product."* He goes on to say that *"a brand is a person's gut feeling about a product, service or organization."* It is an ideal strategy since striking off the negatives paves a more straightforward path for the positives.

And as stated previously, this personal element or rather the gut "feeling" is what creates a pitch for a brand. A brand becomes successful when they succeed in arousing a certain level of attachment in the customer, making them return to the product despite the never-ending list of newer products and brands that invades the market day-by-day. Therefore, we can say that its effect on the customer can define a brand because it precisely becomes the customer's path back to the product.

Another reason for the fuzzy haze surrounding the question, "what is a brand" is its broad scope that cannot be limited by a fixed definition. The additions to the idea of a brand eventually help in the evolution of brand and branding. This fact is attested by the example of using the word "brand" over the years. From a mere naming tool used by cattle ranchers to the idea that dominates skyscrapers and sophisticated products, the evolution has indeed caught up the pace. And there indeed is scope for more. Despite their temporary nature, brands are business tools that drive commercial value.

Think of any brand that pops up in your head first, whether Apple, FedEx, or Coca-Cola. For the sake of consensus, let us consider Apple, given the celebrated brand's vast popularity and reception.

The **Apple** logo does not encompass the entirety of the idea of a "brand." It turns out the Apple brand is not anything in the real sense of the word. You cannot hold it, see it, or touch it. But that does not negate the fact that its brand is the single most valuable thing owned by the company. This "brand" is the reason why you cannot pay or even convince a good majority of apple users to taste or try another brand. Innovation, forward-thinking, flawless experience of the Apple brand has become an inextricable part of a legion of devoted followers' identities. For this reason, its brand is its ultimate competitive advantage. Nothing else can match its stride.

A strong brand improves the possibilities of customers choosing your product or service over your competitors. It not only attracts more customers, but it also lowers the cost per acquisition.

A brand is more than just a logo, it is an embodiment of the most profound principles and values that a brand wishes to convey itself as a representative. And hence, deserves rigorous focus.

Building nonoscillating brand values

How does a single brand have such an impact?

The answer lies in our core—according to anthropologists, humans are hungry for meaning. People use various symbols and structures to build an ever-evolving sense of self. Some of that purpose and meaning is coming from the brands.

Theory of Brand Culture provides a deeper insight. It states that the old model of branding, based on building an external, fictional, brand image, is no longer relevant. People today want honesty and real connection.

Theory of Brand Culture offers an improved model of branding. It proposes that a brand may work like a culture, in the anthropological sense of the word. It uses the Clifford Geertz definition of culture, which is:

"A historically transmitted pattern of meanings embodied in symbols, a system of inherited conceptions expressed in symbolic forms by means of which [humans] communicate, perpetuate, and develop their knowledge about and attitudes towards life."

What does it signify? Well, let us take an example. Suppose a culture—say Hopi Indians—is deep-rooted in a core set of values. A custom of viewing the world, and a way of acting in the world that continues unmodified. This culture has survived hundreds of years of occupation, first by Spaniards and then followed by Americans, all this ought to be credited to the values that have remained consistent. But the same should not be equated to stagnation. The Hopi culture has morphed sufficiently enough to be able to adapt to the gusts of change.

Theory of Brand Culture extends the same philosophy to brands. Based on anthropologists' studies on consumers, this is exactly how a brand should operate. By building brand values that happen to be uniform throughout, a brand allows consumers to contrast those values against their own. When consumers find a brand that compliments their moral fabric, they willingly associate with it. It works fairly similarly with employees.

This is why a brand isn't just a producer of goods and services exclusively. The trend of brands upholding specific principles and values—values that sincerely accelerate every action and conversation, both inside and outside of the brand, has marked its arrival. The trend often reveals itself in a multitude of brand experiences that have successfully displaced the older advertising campaigns.

To better understand why your brand is so valuable, let's start by breaking down its fundamental elements.

The fundamental elements include the brand compass, company culture, name and tagline, identity, voice and messaging, website, and brand architecture.

Brand Compass

The brand compass shows the direction discerned during the strategy phase, thereby helping a company navigate smoothly—it comprises five elements; Purpose, Vision, Mission, Values, and Strategic Objectives.

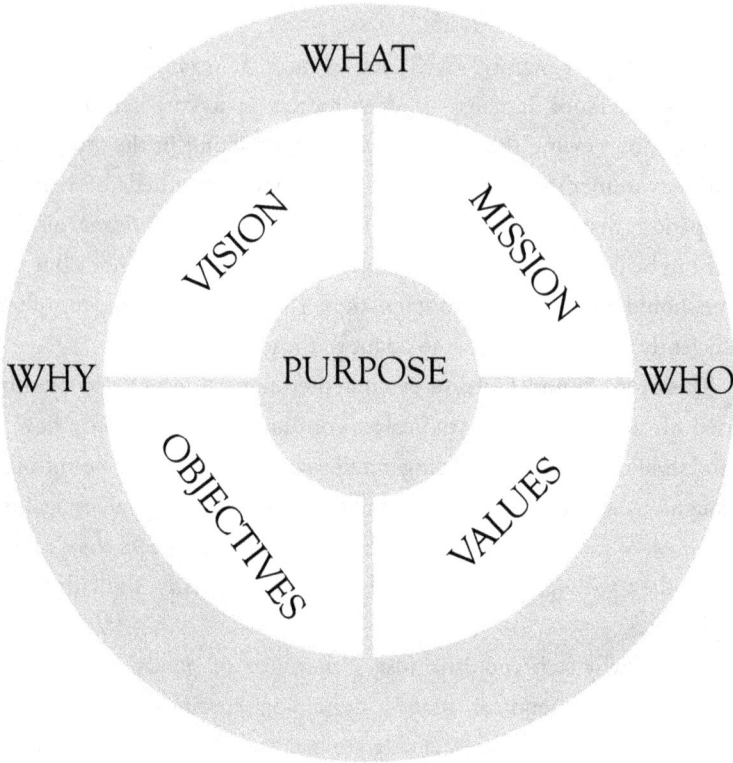

Company Culture

Company culture is the fruit of an idea based on core values and principles that act as lamps on your brand's journey to success. It is a spirit of collective purpose where diverse individuals breathe as one whole with a sole aim. At its deepest level, company culture drives the employees to work with motivation and determination to act as ambassadors and flag bearers of the brand.

Brand Personality

Brand Personality is the streak of unique elements that make its canvas one of a kind. It is the spectrum of thoughts and ideas, and patterns that define a brand at an individual level. It is the key that opens the door to healthy personal relationships with the customers who can identify a particular brand through the connection aroused by its personality.

Brand Architecture

Brand architecture is the coordinated system of names, colors, symbols, and visual language that defines a brand or brands. Superior and advanced brand architecture has its foundation on thorough research to enhance customer experience, and it has to it a particular intentional and intuitive element. Brand architecture systems can be classified as either monolithic, endorsed, or pluralistic. The monolithic brand architecture comprises a particular master brand and multiple sub-brands. Endorsed and pluralistic include parent brands with varying relationships to the divisions over which they preside.

Name and Tagline

Name and tagline is the brand's immediate face, the first sight element that projects the brand to the world, and therefore, it should be treated with utmost care. Naming a brand is not a random process. Instead, much planning, brainstorming, and creativity go in to put forth a name that appeals to the potential customer and captures his attention. The complicated nature of creating words and taglines is a testament to their importance. A firm name conveys a brand's unique value propositions, differentiating it from the competition and leaving a strong impression.

Brand Identity

In simple words, compare the brand identity to that masterstroke of a paintbrush that differentiates a mediocre painting from a masterpiece. A brand identity is more than just a logo but a nutshell that holds within the rich riot of the most profound principles and values upheld by a brand. A brand's identity is the nonerasable mark left by it. It is connected to the visual element, the sense that appeals to a mind before any other.

Voice and Messaging

Voice is what distinguishes and highlights your brand amidst the noise of the world. It is the humanizing factor that creates a strong connection with the customer, turning the brand into an identifiable one. Voice conveys the brand's purpose, promise, and personality in various ways, whether via advertising, marketing collaterals, or website copies. As long as the customer can recognize your brand just like one recognizes an old acquaintance, you can be sure that the "voice" has been heard and the message conveyed.

Brand Website

The website of a brand is the platform where the brand is viewed and experienced with increased clarity. Compelling content and appealing design are the factors that fuel a website to bring the brand to the forefront. With the advent of technology, websites are no longer confined to the desktop. Instead, they open up the world of the brand in every corner of the world, thereby becoming the most impactful and cost-effective ways to deliver a holistic branding experience to your target audience.

A Brand can be viewed as a polychromatic resultant of profuse classic sociology theories: functionalism, conflict theory, and symbolic interactionism.

- **Functionalism**: This as a theory of society underlines the structures that create the society and emphasizes interrelationships that hold the society as an organism of its own, in a stable state. It suggests viewing every group phenomena as an act of holding the society together in some way and looks for the role that phenomena play. Successful brands play a role in gluing society together, for example, Starbucks.
- **Conflict theory**: First purported by Karl Marx, it is a theory that views society from a singular pinhole of perpetual conflict because of competition for limited resources. It identifies with domination and power as a way to maintain social order, instead of consensus and conformity. It states that social phenomena are part of a struggle between exploiter and

exploited; brands are thought to be putting wool over the lower classes' eyes by instigating wants and hence distracting them from their true circumstances.

- **Symbolic interactionism**: This develops from the interplay between the essential self and the socially constructed self (the "I" and the "me"). It posits the notion of people's particular utilization of dialect to designate images and ascribe normal implications, for deduction and correspondence with others in specific circumstances. Brands mediate between these two by serving as carriers of identity and meaning.

Ultimately, what matters is not the "what" part of the question but the "why" and "how." As long as we answer that, we are halfway through the journey with finesse. To simplify this a bit further, let us draw a parallel between a brand and a story's plot. In a story, the plot is a defining element catering to the how, when, where, and why. Similarly, a brand is this defining element that provides a strong connection literally and metaphorically when it comes to a business. Brand simultaneously is one and a whole. And as long as we comprehend this idea, the haze would finally shift, and we will be able to move through the smoke with better clarity.

Key Takeaways

1. *A brand is not an exact science. It is an exhibition of the idea that people are very different and view everything through their own customized filter or perspective. These emotions form a specific connection or loyalty toward a particular product or service.*
2. *A brand is defined as an identifying symbol, mark, logo, name, word, and/or sentence that companies use to distinguish their product from others.*
3. *A brand is all about perception. A brand is a common perception people have developed through direct or indirect interactions, about an organization/products and/or its services.*
4. *Despite their intangible nature, brands are business tools that drive commercial value. It refers not only to the sales and partnerships it brings in but is developed as an asset, which you can find in the financial sheet of a company as "Goodwill."*
5. *A strong brand improves the possibilities of customers choosing your product or service over your competitors. That happens because of their ability to connect with their target audience via their brand identity/ personality/experience.*
6. *The fundamental elements of branding include—the brand compass, company culture, name and tagline, identity, voice and messaging, website, and brand architecture.*
7. *A brand compass is a priceless instrument for outlining a path to your brand's success. It ensures consistent messaging and identity across all touchpoints. A brand compass shows the direction discerned during the strategy phase, thereby helping a company navigate smoothly—it comprises five elements; Purpose, Vision, Mission, Values, and Strategic Objectives.*
8. *Company culture is the fruit of an idea based on core values and principles that act as lamps on your brand's journey to success. It's how employees feel regarding their work, the values they believe in, where they see the business going and what they are doing to get it there.*
9. *Brand personality is the spectrum of thoughts and ideas, and patterns that define a brand at an individual level. It is a set of human characteristics assigned to a particular brand so that the consumer can*

relate to it. Having a uniform set of traits that a targeted user segment can enjoy drives up brand equity in the market.

10. Brand architecture is an orderly formation of the company's collection of brands, sub-brands, and offerings. Its formation systems can be classified as either monolithic, endorsed, or pluralistic.

11. The monolithic brand architecture (also known as Branded House) comprises a particular master brand and multiple sub-brands, for example, for FedEx (FedEx Corporation, FedEx Freight, FedEx Trade Networks, FedEx Ground).

12. The endorsed brand architecture comprises different and unique product brands connected collectively by an endorsing parent brand, for example, Apple (iPad, iTunes, iPhone, iCloud).

13. Pluralistic brand architecture (also known as the house of brands) is a group of apparently independent products, all recognized in their respective demands but limited to none visible connection to the primary parent brand, for example, P&G (Tide, Gillette, Oral-B, Old Spice).

14. A firm name conveys a brand's unique value propositions, differentiating it from the competition and leaving a strong impression.

15. A brand's identity is simply how your brand looks. It is connected to the visual element, the sense that appeals to a mind before any other. The colors, font, design, shapes all fall under a brand identity.

16. Voice conveys the brand's purpose, promise, and personality. The tone of voice and the messaging pull your consumers to understand what you offer and why they need you.

17. The website of a brand is the platform where the brand is viewed and experienced with increased clarity. Compelling content and appealing design are the factors that fuel a website to bring the brand to the forefront.

CHAPTER 2

Overview

In continuation to establishing a brand, this chapter further delves into the process and importance of creating brand awareness. Investopedia defines brand awareness as the "extent to which consumers are familiar with the distinctive qualities or image of a particular brand of goods or services." It is concerned with a brand's position within the customer's mind, regardless of whether it is found on the topmost shelf where it is easily visible and reachable or somewhere along the bottom, mixed with the rest. The chapter continues to explain how in highly saturated markets, lack of brand awareness leads to a business's product/service getting lost in the chaos. Also, discussing Kotler's theory on the effect of brand perception, which is the consumers' ability to identify the brand under different conditions, as reflected by their brand recognition or recall performance. When it comes to brand awareness, there are two essential terms to be kept in mind, which are crucial to understanding the concept: brand recognition and brand recall. The former is defined by a consumer's ability to differentiate a brand from others credited to prior knowledge. Whereas, the latter is based on the ability to recall a particular brand when given the class or category of the product, which can be either done through aided stimulus or top of the mind awareness. It is a slow and gradual process, but the immense value it holds in sustaining a business is explained in detail.

Brand Awareness

A human mind is a beautiful and, at times, complicated spectrum of thoughts and feelings and memories, and many other elements that dwell within the unnamed domain of ideas and imagination. In short, it is a canvas with a vivid and diverse splash of colors. And, we can poetically compare brand awareness to highlighting one specific hue from this blend so that it stands out with a unique glaze and brightness.

Knowledge and familiarity are what pave ways to strengthen relationships and acceptance.

If people don't know you, they wouldn't see the value you add to their life; for instance, think about a flower with pink and golden hues with fragrance better than any perfume, and the healing properties that are beyond this world. It is truly the most useful, unique, and beautiful flower globally, but it blooms and dies in some isolated forest, unknown to the world. Even after having life-saving properties, it is lost and unknown in

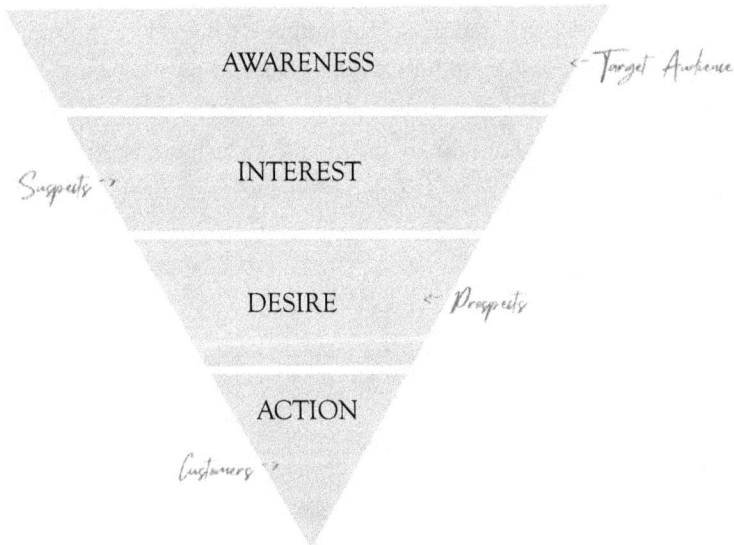

AWARENESS   ← Target Audience

Suspects →   INTEREST

DESIRE   ← Prospects

ACTION

Customers →

oblivion. And that is your brand (product or service) lost in the chaos without brand awareness.

Brand awareness is concerned with a brand's position within the customer's mind, whether it is on the topmost shelf where it is easily visible and reachable or somewhere along the bottom, mixed with the rest. If the situation is the latter, then the brand must focus on developing a better impact on the customer to easily recall the brand to memory and identify it with ease even among the thousands of other names.

Perception is how we see and interpret ourselves and the environment that we inhabit. However, the same isn't always a conscious process. Whatever that ends up being stored within isn't always intentional. Often, our psychology is a result of bits of information that have been consciously or subconsciously ingrained as we experience it, a process we refer to as a perceptual filter. To us, this is reality, though it may not be an accurate account of what actually reality is composed of. Hence, simply put, perception is just the way we filter stimuli (e.g., someone talking to us, reading a book) and then extract sense out of it.

Perception has several steps.

Exposure—Interaction with a stimuli via any sensory organ (e.g., seeing an advertisement)

Attention—An effort to contemplate the nature of a stimuli (e.g., recognizing it is an advertisement of a particular brand)

Awareness—Assigning meaning by rules, schemata, and scripts (e.g., humorous advertisement for particular product)

Retention—Storage of awareness along with pre-existing perceptions in the memory (i.e., brand has fun advertisement)

Brand perception is the sum total of consumers' ability to recognize and recall the brand under different conditions.

When it comes to brand awareness, there are two essential terms to be kept in mind, which are crucial to understanding the concept: **brand recognition** and **brand recall.** Though they seem like favorable terms, which they are to an extent, it is essential to be aware of the thin line of distinction between the two.

Brand recognition can be defined as a customer's ability to recognize prior knowledge of a brand when asked about the brand or their ability to differentiate and identify the brand from the rest. That ability is directly proportional to the product's impact that adheres to personalized service, one defining aspect of brand awareness.

Brand recall is the ability to recall a particular brand when given the class or category of the product, which is similar to what we discussed at the beginning of the chapter about highlighting one specific color or hue from the rest.

There are two types of brand awareness.

- **Aided awareness** is about how the customer recognizes a particular brand when the category pops from a given list of brands.
- **Top of the mind awareness** or immediate brand recall means the reach of a brand whose impact is quite vital that it is the first name that rushes to the customers' mind on mentioning the product category. For example, when talking about soft drinks, involuntarily, a good majority of people think about Coca-Cola. That is one good example of brand awareness done right.

The importance of brand awareness in a business's growth underscores customers' part in a product's success. And, to build better brand awareness, it is vital to understand the likes and dislikes and the choices of a potential customer. **Rather than treating customers as a stepping stone to the throne of success, consider them a part of the family whose presence is of utmost importance in completing and making it whole.** If established successfully, this connection will be reflected in the producer–consumer relationship, as well, as it goes a long way in taking the business to the forefront. Because ultimately, the success of a brand lies in the understanding that customers are crucial and significant assets to the company and investing in them always gives the best return.

Brand awareness or, for that matter, building brand awareness does not happen overnight. It is not an abrupt decision made on a whim.

Instead, it is a well-thought-out and planned strategy with a strong foundation of brand building strategy. When it comes to developing brand awareness, there is no lack of choices, which is a boon and bane at the same time. Because when there are plenty of options, choosing the right one with prudence determines success. And, brand strategists must pay careful attention so that this first step does not go wrong.

There are various diverse channels, as mentioned earlier, like advertising, word-of-mouth publicity, social media, sponsorships, launching events, and many more. And, it is vital to have a close eye on the customer preferences and trends to employ the right channel. If this, one can add a streak of innovation and creativity that can help the brand stand out, it becomes closer to success.

And another critical factor to be kept in mind is the **consistency of the message that the brand intends to communicate** with the customer because though the trends keep changing, it is essential to adapt and innovate while at the same time maintaining a firm ground on the fundamental ideal or message. Because for a building to be sturdy, it should have a fixed and robust foundation that does not waver or shake.

Coca-Cola in Mexico is a quintessential example for the same. The case study goes as follows:

When Mexico Coca-Cola apprehended diminished popularity among millennials, they sought to develop a campaign to raise awareness and improve brand perception. The "Share a Coke" campaign sign had already been a global success, so the brand decided to adapt it for a younger audience. The campaign was launched in a new avatar as a mobile campaign that would target Mexican teens and young adults. However, the technological accessibility and mobile experiences are not uniform in distribution within the Mexican population, especially the youth, but are based on individual household income. While some have a high-end mobile experience, others hardly can pay for Wi-Fi. Despite this, Coca-Cola aspired to reach around 22 million Mexican millennials.

For this, they adopted a creative strategy targeting teens and young adults. The display advertising for the "Share a Coke" brand awareness campaign required to be innovative, focusing on capturing attention and stimulation of emotions to connect with their audience. That's what was reflected in the unique, unprecedented execution; they adopted brilliant implementation techniques. Coca-Cola eyed the top 100 searches on YouTube and created short ads with the names of the most-searched artists, athletes, and trending YouTubers. It also showed pre-roll ads that included personalized cans with names of the actors and characters.

Additionally, they created banners for Yahoo!, which were personalized for each user and so much so that they were optimized in real time. It also used brand search knowledge marketing to formulate a marketing campaign in which, when a person who explored a Bruno Mars song on YouTube could "Share a Coke" with him.

It is vital to appreciate that Coca-Cola created a campaign specifically for a Mexican audience, so the ideas were backed by a strong cultural sensibility because of a good understanding of Mexicans and specifically Mexican millennial culture. Although, reaching a broad audience with varying degrees of mobile needs was a daunting task. Nevertheless, Coca-Cola was successful, utilizing YouTube, the second biggest online channel and the No. 1 entertainment reference in Mexico, as its platform.

This campaign increased the brand awareness of Coca-Cola, helping them connect with millennials. By leveraging technology and insights of the high usage of YouTube used by young people, the music streaming service with targeted developed content reminded millennials to share a Coke with their friends.

As a result, 1.7 million new users reached 175 million social media views and 3.2 million views for the TV commercial. Additionally, there was 51 percent of website traffic from mobile devices, and 44 percent of Mexico shared a Coke. The campaign acclaimed a groundbreaking success in brand awareness.

A brand must stay consistent so that consumers can depend on it.

Every communication or marketing campaign with your consumers should be monitored to make it relevant to the brand personality. It has to be consistent and portray the correct brand image year after year. And, it's harder than it sounds, because maybe you hired a new agency or a change of marketing personnel who wants to make their mark by "exploring new routes." Do not make a change for the sake of change.

If your social media posts are bright colors and silly but your product packaging is muted and plain, you are sending mixed signals that will confuse consumers and leave them feeling like your brand can't be trusted. According to LucidPress, the average revenue increase that attributes to brand consistency is more than 20 percent and consistent brand colors can increase recognition by up to 80 percent.

A brand is a living organism that evolves with the push of external, social, environmental factors, just like us humans, but the foundational values endure. Staying true to your moral compass while having a controlled natural evolution of your brand results in a timeless brand. I wish to encapsulate this essence and call it the Chahat's evolution of brand theory (CEB theory). When we push a brand into an unnatural direction for a sake of change, an unsavory result is to be expected. The same result is to be expected when we defy evolution and are unwilling to adapt. The answer to a successful brand is simple—keeping the core value consistent and letting it evolve naturally with time makes an impact!

Let's see this theory in action, how Dove became the world's leading cleansing brand while staying consistent for more than 60 years!

Dove started with the launch of the Dove Beauty Bar in the 1950s. It revolutionized the method women cared for their skin. Dove grew as a brand because in all these years, their personality and identity stayed the same—"Dove doesn't dry your skin the way soap can." Many of the ads featured the image of cream being poured into the Dove bar to emphasize its moisturizing quality—this signature image still remains a staple today.

In the 1950s, it communicated the facial moisturizing benefits of the product, with the introduction of the Dove Face Test campaign. In the late 1960s, Dove first began to use "real women" in its advertising and reiterated the brand's nondrying benefit into the 1970s. Dove cream-pouring images continued to anchor the spots, but the tagline changed from "one-quarter cleansing cream" to "one-quarter moisturizing cream," keeping the key offering and purpose of the brand unchanged.

They continued to strengthen its original message that Dove won't dry your skin, adding research to back up the claim. Either with a litmus paper test or a "seven-day, feel the difference test." In the late 1980s, communication changed to a detailed account of how Dove has improved a woman's self-esteem as well as her skin—this was the first change toward promoting inner beauty, which it continues to do even today.

Since then, Dove evolved to a brand that believes that beauty should be for everyone, because when you look and feel your best, you feel better about yourself. In the 2000s, The Campaign for Real Beauty was launched after a major global study that revealed that only 2 percent of women around the world would describe themselves as beautiful. This sparked a global conversation about the need for a wider definition of beauty.

"Fifty years ago, women were just looking at product benefits," says MacLeod. "Today they want to affiliate themselves with brands that are doing something good."

In 2020, Dove is the world's leading cleansing brand, with sales of over four billion USD a year in more than 80 countries. And, earning the brand value to 6.51 billion USD. Even though the Dove bar remains unchanged and the nondrying strategy continues to sell the product, today, it markets itself as a social activist.

A fitting example of how if something is working successfully, you don't need to change it. Dove's offering remains the same; however their approach evolved with changing times.

Investopedia defines brand awareness as the **"extent to which consumers are familiar with the distinctive qualities or image of a particular brand of goods or services."** This is a good take-off point when building brand awareness—a frame to fix the canvas in place. In simple terms, just like a name is vital to a person, logos and symbols and phrases are essential to brands, hence the extreme focus and level of brainstorming present when choosing a name or logo. Though it might seem like a trivial step, it amounts to a lot. Because when it comes to brand awareness, every single step adds up, and therefore, we must pay attention to the slightest nuances and subtleties. Just like the much-used phrase suggests, *it is the little things that matter.*

Key Takeaways

1. *The human mind is a complex phenomenon that interprets and perceives different things in unique ways.*
2. *Every individual has their own set of thoughts they have been conditioned with, allowing them to imagine, form ideas and opinions.*
3. *Familiarity with brands is a critical factor in strengthening relationships and overall acceptance.*
4. *Authenticity and straightforward methods to spread knowledge of your brand ensure that people know the value you add to their lives.*
5. *Investopedia defines brand awareness as the "extent to which consumers are familiar with the distinctive qualities or image of a particular brand of goods or services."*
6. *Brand awareness is critical to driving brand recall in a consumer's mind regardless of the place or situation your product is found. Two concepts to remember here are aided understanding and top-of-the-mind recall.*
7. *Brand recognition reflects your product's impact on the customer, based on their ability to identify or differentiate it from others. So, top-of-the-mind awareness is a quantifier of how consumers rank your brand.*
8. *Brand recall refers to the case of when and how consumers find themselves reminiscing about your brand. Aided awareness is how well the customer recognizes your brand when introduced to a particular category.*
9. *It is rightly said that "customer is king." Hence, to build brand awareness, remember to first set your foot to understand potential customers' present and evolving choices.*
10. *A critical factor to be kept in mind is the consistency of the message that the brand intends to communicate with the customer because though the trends keep changing, it is essential to adapt and innovate while at the same time maintaining a firm ground on the fundamental ideal or message.*
11. *Building brand awareness must be a well-thought-out and planned strategy with a strong foundation. It can, indeed, be a slow process. However, choosing the right path in the early stages determines success.*
12. *Channels that can be used include advertising, word-of-mouth publicity, social media, sponsorships, launching events, influencer marketing, and so on.*

13. *The brand must focus on developing a better impact on the customer to easily recall the brand to memory and identify it with ease even among the thousands of other names.*

14. ***Aided awareness*** *is about how the customer recognizes a particular brand when the category pops from a given list of brands.*

15. ***Top-of-the-mind awareness*** *or immediate brand recall means the reach of a brand whose impact is quite vital that it is the first name that rushes to the customers' mind on mentioning the product category. For example, when talking about soft drinks, involuntarily, a good majority of people think about Coca-Cola. That is one good example of brand awareness done right.*

16. *In an extremely dynamic environment, brand authenticity and consistency in tone of voice and messaging are crucial throughout all communications because it generates trust.*

17. *Keep an eye on all the small details, from the brand's name, logo, symbols, voice, taglines, and overall style to the larger picture.*

CHAPTER 3

Overview

The focus of this chapter is to provide an understanding of the impact that branding can have on consumer decisions and how any business must use it to yield the benefits. Beginning with describing the age-old and most popularly known brand—Shakespeare, suggested that marketers have to go beyond the various influences on buyers and build an understanding of how consumers make their buying decisions. The ability to create a good service and to persuade the market to buy this offering depends upon the insight into the consumer purchase decision. A brand's name is its reputation and goodwill, and utilizing the right strategies and tools to market is essential to exhibit the value it provides to consumers. A deeper discussion on the positive outcomes branding has on recognition and image, competition, advertising, investments, revenue along demand and supply. The chapter then converses on the impact good branding has on the internal aspects of a business including trust, crisis mitigation, and employee motivation, which in return can have extraordinary and long-lasting benefits. Both consumers and stakeholders are knowledgeable and conscious about where they invest their time and money, and with a short span of attention, making the first impression sets the right standard.

Brand to Business

What's in a name? That which we call a rose
By any other name would smell as sweet.

—Said Romeo to Juliet

This statement by the dead poet Shakespeare is as ironic as it is thought-provoking. None of us would have been familiar, let alone pondered upon this question of a name for centuries if Shakespeare's brand name didn't market it. This writing business in general and the quote, in particular, could reach you and me because "name," albeit nothing intrinsic in it, sells. What was Shakespeare but a successful business with fantastic marketing and branding?

So, what is in a brand name, and how can it impact your business?
We live in an era of flux where there is nothing constant but change. Technology is ever advancing. Now, the consumer has potent tools at his disposal; these are the tools to create knowledge and awareness. The game-changer for the branding business has proved to be the adaptability to such advancements. If exploited in the right way, technology can lead to the skyrocketing of profits or impede those who are reluctant to change. In this game of marketing, where there are gainers, there are bound to be losers.

Moreover, technology and globalization are intricately woven together in the market that shapes today's economic landscape. Due to globalization blur and the interconnections in the 21st century world, Boundaries of nations are rendered ineffective. This reach implies that there is nothing holding back your brand. The pivot of the game, here, is the reach. "Reach" is not physical but to the consumer's mind. Your marketplace today is the whole big world. Thanks to the online and offline technologies, growth potential today knows no limit other than imagination.

Consumer Decision Making

Mahatoo (1985) interprets consumer behavior or decision-making procedure existing of numerous rests that inaugurate before the involvement and achieve beyond the buying statute. He suggests that marketers have to go beyond the various significance of buyers and improve an understanding of how consumers make their buying judgments.

Price is one of the dominating components when it comes to making a purchase judgment. It generally squirms a critical role in deducing a consumer's brand intent while choosing a product. Consumers look into the price while giving rise to a buying decision and check whether it is within their acceptable bounds. This helps them to maximize the immediate utility that they earn from the purchase. It is understood that customers evaluate the subsequent aid and freebies that come along with the commodity. Customers are supposed to weigh on every characteristic when it comes to the examination technique. The customers who have experienced terrible consumer service tend to investigate all the aspects of the product (Andreassen and Olsen 2008).

According to Kotler (2003), there are five purposes people play during a purchase.

Initiator: It is the person who gives the idea of the product or assistance.
Influencer: It is the person who influences the judgment.
Decider: It is the person who gives a jump to the buying decision: what to buy, how to buy, when to buy, and where to buy.

CONSUMER RETENTION AND LOYALTY

CUSTOMERS WILLING TO PAY MORE

EASY EXPANSION AND EXTENSIONS

HIGHER MARKET SHARE

BRAND BENEFITS

DRIVE MORE CONVERSIONS AND SALES

SALE SALE SALE **SALE**

INCREASED TRUST AND EMOTIONAL CONNECT

INCREASED BUSINESS VALUE

INCREASED TRUST AND EMOTIONAL CONNECT

Buyer: It is the person who invests.

User: It is the person who expends or utilizes the product or assistance. So, while purchasing products and services in an open, competitive market, what exactly drives a consumer's decisions? Branding is not only an essential impression making tool but also works as a standard-setter.

It serves two primary purposes: *firstly*, identifying your brand or product in contrast to all the other consumables and services out in the market, and *secondly*, a uniformity in expectations; your consumers and clients know what to expect from your business. In addition to it, branding has a multitude of takeaways.

Key Benefits From Branding

Recognition and Image

Branding is telling your consumers what to do (i.e., purchase from you) and making it succinct and exciting. For this, image building through a narrative is essential. Potential customers (even before they make purchases from you) are your audience accessing what you have got to give them. It's an audience that is consuming the same narrative of recognition that leads to image building. A worthy image creates goodwill in the market, which in turn secures your position as a dominant player and ultimately "the profit-maker."

> *CEO of the brand Quaker referring to his company, rightly put it, "If the business splits up and I give you the land, bricks, and cement, and take the goodwill and trademarks, I'd still stand better than you."*

A business comprises the tangibles (brick, mortar, land, goods, and more). It is the recognition of a brand by a broader audience that makes it what it is.

Competitiveness

A market segment dominated by a well-known brand becomes almost a no-go zone for new competitors; it is just tough to penetrate deep for the other times. If your business is unique, and you are successfully able to convey that through marketing, you will attract the business environment in which competitors will not compete. Also, establishing brand and brand credibility makes customers turn to you before they go anywhere else. So, even if there are multiple players, good branding will make sure they never have your share of the market.

Trust

Genuine and widely known brands are perceived as less risky to purchase. In turn, this trust leads to a better-marketed perception, and hence, popular products give better performance or are worth the value. Intensely marketed products generate high profits and are proven by the results. Therefore, we can safely assume that the more rigorously you market, the more successful it gets. Branding is nothing but shouting out loud to your customers the reasons to trust you. Your product/service quality might start the process. But, it is your brand that reminds your customers all the time with whom their trust lies and should lie.

Easy Advertisement

It is essential to realize the potential consumer does not have unlimited time or even interest. The onus of letting them know what you are about to offer them lies on you. One must answer all the questions. What expedites the process is, again, your brand. Building a brand identity is paramount with a powerful logo, strong repute, distinct identity, and more. Advertisement falls in line. What follows after that is a deep impression on the consumer.

Revenue

Clients readily pay a premium for products from a well-known brand compared to a similar product from a brand that isn't as well known.

Beyond monetary benefits, an established brand makes customers its success partners as they become regulars. The revenue outlets of such brands are not only sustainable but also ever-increasing in number and volume. Take, for instance; Apple products are notorious for their high prices. What Apple charges you is way more than the actual cost that goes into the effect. The premium that Apple earns is famously called the "Apple tax." This high revenue is possible for Apple because of its brand name, which has become synonymous with high-end technology and durability.

Crisis Mitigation

The market is a perilous landscape. The damaged perception among the audience directly affects sales. A series of or even a couple of mishaps can give your product an unreliable tag. The market is all about image building. In a crisis of perception, it is branding that comes to your rescue. Take, for example, Toyota, which is indeed a brand known for its quality. Unfortunately, back in 2009, there were quality issues reported in some of the products. This incident proved to be a nightmare to the company's public relations (PR). Such a crisis can be mitigated only through years of emphasis on "quality" in all its branding and advertisement campaigns to follow. Toyota, advertising its brand was formerly known for, was soon back to its glory.

Investment

Investors always inject money into famous, strong, worthy enough to hold an audience, and genuine enough to gain their trust. It is generally seen that weak brands struggle to get the adequate investments they need. When a brand is soft, it shows a potential risk; there are fewer chances of willing investors to put in funds. When you invest in your company's branding efforts, outside investment is bound to follow.

Demand and Supply

Being a large firm also results in being the biggest customer of the major suppliers to your business. In this scenario, the suppliers would want to secure their demand, and therefore, they will never want to lose you. This consistent demand and need prove to be a great advantage and can ensure quality products and timely delivery. The power to bargain over the prices comes as the cherry on the top. Suppliers might accept a pay cut to keep supplying your company. A famous brand with customer loyalty faces lesser issues discovering distribution partners on a local and global scale. Distributors, suppliers, and the entire demand–supply web would work efficiently with a brand where a positive brand repute stabilizes the client demand.

Employees

A renowned brand attracts the best brains. When your brand is well-known, people will want to work for you. This brand pull is a cycle of growth. Good marketing equals popularity; popularity brings the brain, the brain generates profit, profit means investment, and the process goes on. When employees work for such a brand, they showcase a sense of loyalty. As a result, the employees are there to stay. Not only this, the employees are going to give out their best because they believe in what their company is doing and are proud of the name it has earned.

It is understood that spending on banding, in the longer run, has limitless incentives in growth. However, the most important thing to focus on is the proper execution of your branding strategy to make the right impact on the target audience.

Key Takeaways

1. *Your brand's name is your reputation and goodwill, so using the right strategy and tools to market, it is essential to exhibit the value it provides.*

2. *Ever-growing technology can be a boon or bane, depending on how fast one adapts to newfound trends and preferences will either increase or crash profits.*

3. *Technology and globalization are interdependent, shaping today's economic landscape. International boundaries have now become as permeable as consumer's minds—increasing market size and enormous potential customer base on a global scale.*

4. *Both online and offline technology work together to offer boundless growth opportunities.*

5. *Consumers today are much more knowledgeable and conscious about where they invest their time and money, and with a short span of attention, making the first impression sets the right standard.*

6. *Analyzing your brand product in contrast to all the other consumables and services already available in the market helps identify your brand's sweet spot in a saturated market.*

7. *Branding has numerous benefits and helps create a set of expectations in terms of the quality and experience for your consumers.*

8. *Price is one of the dominating components when it comes to making a purchase judgment. It generally squirms a critical role in deducing a consumer's brand intent while choosing a product.*

9. *There are five purposes people play during a purchase—initiator, influencer, decider, buyer, and user.*

10. *Recognition and image—Powerful branding involves creating substantial goodwill through storytelling. It allows potential customers to be acquainted with your brand even before they experience it and keeps them hooked to come back, making you a winner. Wide audience recognition is what maintains the longevity of any brand.*

11. *Competitiveness—Entering dominated market segments can be challenging. Creating a unique and credible brand ensures customers always pick you over all the multiple players in the market landscape.*

12. *Trust—What segregates well-known brands from others is the perception of less risk and better quality. The right and consistent marketing strategy acts as a reminder to your consumers to keep their trust intact with your product/services.*

13. *Easy advertisement—Once a prominent brand identity has been built with a powerful logo, strong reputation, distinct identity, and personality, advertising continues to keep consumers hooked to your brand on an emotional level.*

14. *Revenue—It is a known fact that consumers are willing to pay higher prices for well-known brands over unknown ones despite comparatively better value at quality and price. An established brand makes customers its success partners, and such brands' revenue outlets are sustainable and ever-increasing in number and volume.*

15. *Crisis mitigation—A market is a dangerous place because of its dynamic nature and the lasting adverse effects a damaged perception can directly have on reputation and sales. Having a strong brand can result in high support in negating and surviving through PR nightmares.*

16. *Investment—Investing in powerful branding attracts investors to inject money into your brand. It provides them with faith that their money is in a worthy set up to grow and give them high return on investment (ROI).*

17. *Demand and supply—Having an established firm results in long-term contracts with suppliers with consistent quality, timely deliveries, and better pricing. Distributors, suppliers, and the entire demand–supply web would work efficiently with a brand where a positive brand reputation stabilizes the client demand.*

18. *Employees—Every individual dreams of being part of a great organization; hence, investing in good brand values and culture attracts the best talent. In return, this continues to give the company multifold benefits and growth.*

CHAPTER 4

Overview

The value and importance of branding have been emphasized in the previous few chapters, but the aspect that grabs business attention is the final output in terms of profit and return on investment (ROI). This chapter deals exactly with this, starting with a short success story that was built on the value of emotions and aesthetics. Existing notions on the prerequisites for branding are clarified by explaining the ratio between the investment and actual business returns with effective branding. The chapter moves on defining brand equity, and some of the models of brand equity suggested by researchers including the (i) Aaker model that deals with brand loyalty, brand awareness, perceived quality, brand associations, and proprietary assets; (ii) brand asset valuator (BAV) model, with four components, including differentiation, relevance, esteem, knowledge; and (iii) BrandZ model, which discusses a chronological set of steps, including focusing on presence, relevance, and performance, advantages, and bonding. The reader is then provided with a deeper understanding of how branding generates ROI with examples, case studies, and factors that determine ROI in terms of qualitative and quantitative measurements. Some of the qualitative aspects described are financial value, customer value, process value, and cultural value.

Brand ROI

Great things are done by a series of small things brought together
—Vincent Van Gogh

Van Gogh, the famous painter, today, was doomed to a life of obscurity as we know him. He lived his life in abjure poverty. But, his fame (posthumous) is a quintessential example of branding.

After Vincent 's death, his brother Theo wanted to win his brother's recognition. But, just six months after Vincent's death, Theo passed away.

Theo's widow, Jo van Gogh-Bogner, set about the task of marketing Vincent's work. She not only sold some of Vincent's works, gave others out for exhibitions but also, very importantly, published his letters to Theo. What sells, even now, is Van Gogh's fascinating life story. Gradually his work took the whole world by storm; this could happen only because of very calculated consumer influence not just stemming from aesthetic value but—more importantly, emotive values.

The preconceived notion that branding requires a fortune does not always hold. There are myriad ways to market your company

Branding Channels: PUBLIC RELATIONS, CONTEST, SIGNAGE, WORD OF MOUTH, BUSINESS CARDS, NETWORKING, LETTERHEAD, BLOGS, SOCIAL MEDIA, VOICE MESSAGES, PROMOTION, SAMPLE, SPONSORS, PUBLICATIONS, ADVERTISING, TRADE SHOW, EXHIBITS, ENVIRONMENT, E-MAIL, TELEPHONE, BILLBOARD, WEB BANNERS, VEHICLES, PRESENTATION, EXPERIENCES, WEBSITE, PACKAGING, SERVICES, SOCIAL, BUSINESS FORMS, EMPLOYEES, SPEECHES, DIRECT MAIL, PRODUCTS in a cost-efficient and effective manner (e.g., online marketing). The unconventional marketing ways at hand-cut costs amplify the outreach, making it possible to reach a wider audience. Many alternative forms of customer education are available at hand. These methods (such as a tie-up with online marketing platforms) can educate customers and clients about special deals, promotions, discounts, and other new offerings. Not to mention, such an offering is in itself a proven marketing strategy.

Furthermore, the paucity of funds is not the reason great enough to compromise on marketing or efforts. When convinced of the benefits, a business can look out for easy and quick loans, which are very common these days.

Nonetheless, there is one thing to keep in mind when it comes to marketing: **ROI**. In simpler words, every penny you put as an investment should create an appropriate value (appropriate ROI). ROI is a standard business jargon used to identify past and potential financial returns. So, why does an endeavor need to be assessed by the ROI it generates? Simply because this measure indicates how successful a venture will be. Often a simple percentage or ratio, the ROI of endeavor, aids the decision making (by managers and executives of a firm). As to invest in a particular thing or the other, taking into account, every expenditure has an opportunity cost.

Calculate ROI by any business expense done on acquiring the customer. Not all costs incurred generate a tangible ROI. For instance,

Branding Benefits

Customer Recognition

Customer Loyalty

Credibility

Gives Confidence

Consistency

Brand Equity

Attracts Talent

Allows Shared Values

repairing an elevator shaft or buying a new coffee machine, for that matter, cannot be considered as a direct ROI expenditure of even an investment. However, these expenses generate some overarching benefit. On the other hand, expenses like upgrading the company's website and hiring a content creator for ads can be considered ROI.

No matter how big, no firm has an unlimited marketing budget. A firm or business has to consider both the long-term goal and the short-term budgeting target before making any branding expenditure decisions.

ROI is also used to describe "opportunity cost" or a return that investors gave up to invest in the company. In simpler words, the cost of doing a sure thing and not doing the other instead.

In the microcosm that is the branding world, all the efforts are poured into generating the ultimate ROI in terms of brand equity.

Let's dive in to understand what it is, how it is evaluated and accumulated?

Brand equity, shorn of any jargon, is the added value conferred to products and services. Aaker (1991) defined brand equity as a set of brand assets and liabilities associated with a brand that either inflate or deflate the value extracted from a product or service based upon customers' perspectives. The same may be reflected in how consumers think, feel, and act concerning the brand.

Brand equity is a significant intangible asset that has both psychological and financial value to the firm. Its value relies upon the number of people who happen to buy a product repeatedly (Aaker 1996). All three—brand loyalty, brand awareness, and brand perceived quality—are vital to maintaining brand equity (Motameni and Shahrokhi 1998). The two different perspectives of brand equity are: financial and customer-based. The former appraises the asset value of a brand name (Farquhar et al. 1991). Financial perspective measures the magnitude of brand equity by the increase in the discounted future cash flows and revenue compared to a similar product that did not possess the brand name (Motameni and Shahrokhi 1998).

The customer-based approach emphasizes the fact that the powers of a brand are based upon factors such as how a customer responds, views, reads, hears, learns, thinks, and feels about it over a course of time. In layman's terms, the power of a brand is what is in the minds of existing or potential customers and what they have experienced directly or indirectly about the brand. It is the customer-based brand equity that eventually results in the financial return to the company (Lassar et al. 1995). The valuation of a brand has been studied for different approaches, for instance, marketing, premium pricing market value, customer factors, replacement cost perspective. According to the valuation based on consumer factors, the measurement of customers' preferences and attitudes can be utilized to evaluate brand equity (Aaker 1991 and Kapferer 1992).

Types of Brand Equity Models

1. **Aaker model**

   Aaker model defines brand equity as a group of assets and liabilities that can be directly associated with the brand and that which adds value to the product. The model put forward by Professor David Aaker is a combination of five components.

   Brand loyalty

   This measures the tendency of a customer to buy a product faithfully regardless of the availability of other options.

   Brand awareness

   This is the extent to which the brand is recalled and/or recognized in the market.

   Perceived quality

   This relates to the overall quality or superiority of a product in the minds of the intended customers.

   Brand associations

   This refers to the extent to which the product has been ingrained in the mind of a consumer.

   Proprietary assets

   This enlists all kinds of patents, intellectual property rights, trademarks, and so on that are in the possession of a brand.

   These components of the Aaker model coalesce to shape a customer's choice. A customer will be keen to associate with a brand that ensures superior quality and satisfaction.

2. **Brand asset valuator (BAV) model**

BAV is a brand equity model that has been utilized to estimate the brand equity value of innumerable brands and has also been used as a tool to compare the same across many brands. As per the model, accumulating consumer insights helps boost brand health presently as well as in the future.

The four prime components of brand equity under the BAV model are:

Differentiation

As the name suggests, it refers to the ability of a brand to have a distinct individuality of its own. It is an index of uniqueness.

Relevance

Relevance as a concept is a byproduct of appeal, which in turn can be ascertained by questioning relevance to customers in terms of the cost, the fulfillment of needs, convenience, and so on.

Esteem

Esteem is the admiration held by the consumers for a product for its sheer quality and superior performance metrics over its competitors. It can also be viewed as a barometer of the consumers' response to the growing popularity of the brand or the decline of the brand.

Knowledge

This measures the level of familiarity of the consumer with a specific brand. It is the eventual aim of all brand-building exercises undertaken.

The BAV model attempts to find threads of interrelationships among differentiation, relevance, esteem, and knowledge to determine the strength of a brand.

3. **BrandZ model**

Developed by two marketing research consultants, Millward Brown and WPP, BrandZ is a tool to envisage brand equity. In this model, data used is gleaned from two major sources—interviews and publicly available information. Consumers of different brands are asked questions about the brands that they happen to be familiar with.

As per this model, brand building is based on five sequential steps. The steps are not interchangeable, and of course, the success of each step in this model is based upon the one preceding it.

Presence—Do I know about it?
This is a stage of building active recall value of the product based on past trials and brand promise.

Relevance—Does it offer me something?
Once familiarity is established, the next step in the process is of relevance. Does the product offer what consumers want? Does the product effectively fulfill the gap that caused the need to arise in the first place?

Performance—Can it deliver?
Once the product is known to hold relevance in consumers' life, the next step is to ensure that the product delivers on what it promises. Is the performance or experience the same as expected or as promised? The better the performance, the better the brand equity.

Advantages—Does it offer something better than others?
Once the product is known to deliver what it has promised, the next step is to find out if the product has been able to carve a distinct bond with the consumer or attain a preference over the other close substitutes available in the market.

Bonding—Nothing else beats it.
This is the final step where the product has proved to be excellent and has built a strong bond with the user. This shall weed out all other competing products because the customer is now sentimentally as well as psychologically inclined to the product and hence is not ready to substitute it with any other option available.

An ample amount of brand equity models have been formulated by a lot of researchers to study and comprehend consumer behavior. These models have proved to be a sturdy means to attain the same.

Now that you have a grasp over the foundational variables, let's have a look at the nebulous concept of how they interact.

How Branding Generates ROI?

Take, for example, an advertising campaign. To calculate its ROI, the investor would analyze the sales increased after the advertisement campaign and use that information in his calculation. If the money thus generated exceeds the amount spent, a business could consider it a positive ROI.

We can understand the benefits of marketing by evaluating the "brand-building ROI."

Traditionally, the brand-building ROI was calculated by subtracting all the costs incurred from profits and dividing it by the value.

Although this ROI, based on quantitative metrics, gives us a broader picture, if you solely consider this method, you might miss out on many insights on adjusting future investments in such marketing campaigns. It might also, at times, be unsuccessful in showing how people engage with your brand. ***Looking at the ROI from brand-building activities, one should look at both qualitative and quantitative measurements.***

Some qualitative aspects for the same are:

Financial Value

It is the contribution made by brand building to your company's financial results. Also, brand valuation is done periodically by various valuation firms, which is the company's net present value. It also includes other things such as price premium paid on brand products, miscellaneous charges such as those on your brand royalty and franchise.

Customer Value

It's about your customer perception of your brand vis-a-vis the others. Also, the larger critical say on differentiation, relevance, esteem, and knowledge of your brand. To some extent (to the extent measurable), customer response.

Process Value

The brand makes a business run more efficiently. It substantially improves the organizational process, including the standard business processes like hiring employees, managing the supply chain, and creating successful campaigns quicker and hassle-free. This competence happens due to the strong brand building and generates ROI.

Culture Value

A brand worth of its name creates a great work culture in its office premises. Employees who are proud of the brand's perception are motivated to work efficiently. An employee from a famous brand will love to use and flaunt the merchandise, increasing brand awareness. There is always a sense of pride associated with such a work environment. All this positivity generates efficiency and hence ROI.

> Thanks to the increased data and analytic capabilities at hand today, all these and a lot more can be measured and analyzed. Reiterating the crux of this discussion, the brand has many spillover effects. It leads to ROI that is tangible and visible and that which is not.

Case Study of Effective ROI Generation by Brands

Millar, a growing medical technology-producing company, wanted to go to new levels to get their message to a larger audience. They decided to focus on insight, innovation, and collaboration as the critical elements of the campaign. They needed a global presence to include a far-flung population of medical professionals who wanted the latest cutting-edge and innovative technologies. They did the same investing in their branding. They reaped a latent ROI by creating a strong customer base, which leads to an increase in audience, and their global branding goal was achieved. This case shows that ROI is not always quantifiable in the short term. Its benefits might only be reaped in a long time, and that too latent.

Comcast is another brand that shows the importance of branding. Comcast conducted a study to see how they could better their brand. By creating a classic with a large red "C" around another C and black lettering in the rest of the brand name, the logo gives the message in a minimal and sublime way. Along with this, investing in social media and extensive customer support to build the brand also worked wonders for the brand. The ROI of the last two investments is explicitly vast.

The aforementioned two case studies show that branding is an ROI-generating activity. Its potency should not be underestimated.

Key Takeaways

1. *Branding efforts do not have to cost a fortune. If you cannot do great things, then consider doing small things in a great way.*
2. *There is a plethora of cost-efficient, conventional, and unconventional marketing methods that can effectively educate consumers about special deals, promotions, discounts, and other new offerings. Companies can successfully execute these initiatives with online and offline channels.*
3. *The value of marketing efforts is so high that even scarcity of funds must not compromise its benefits as businesses can seek the option of loans.*
4. *ROI measures the success and worth of the precious resources that have been invested in your venture. In simple terms, it is the revenue and profits that have been generated.*
5. *You should calculate ROI in terms of expenses incurred in the process of acquiring customers.*
6. *Not every business-associated cost is responsible for generating tangible ROI; however, investing in the overall betterment of the organization's facilities and culture positively does contribute indirectly to better ROI.*
7. *As funds are limited, it is crucial to consider both long- and short-term goals while distributing the budget targets for branding expenditure.*
8. *Opportunity cost is an important term to remember, which can be defined as the cost of declining an opportunity to follow through with another.*
9. *Calculating ROI is not very direct but somewhat analytical. The increase or decrease in revenue after implementing specific campaigns can help determine positive or negative returns.*
10. *Brand-building ROI is calculated by subtracting all the costs incurred from profits and dividing it by the value.*
11. *Quantitative metrics are not always the best judge of success, as they cannot showcase qualitative value, which must be analyzed on a broader scale. Hence, both must be considered.*
12. *Financial value is the contribution of brand-building efforts to your company's financial returns.*
13. *Customer value can be measured in terms of the ranking and perception your brand has on consumers, which leads to repeated buying.*

14. *Process value—Organized systems and processes ensure the business's smooth running from managing human resource (HR) and supply chains to creative initiatives, which only adds to positive ROI.*

15. *Culture value—Happy employees equal a happy business. Investing in company culture and initiatives to keep employees engaged and proud of their organization plays a huge role in any organization's overall performance.*

16. *Technology has contributed to faster and efficient analytic capabilities, allowing organizations to run models through algorithms to understand the best ROI generating opportunities even before spending a penny.*

17. *Millar's focus on insight, innovation, and collaboration proves that ROI is not always quantifiable in the short term but instead experienced with patience in a long time. On the contrary, Comcast's minor logo tweaks and heavy digital marketing did wonders for the brand in a shorter period.*

CHAPTER 5

Overview

Now that the concept of a brand is clear, it is time to magnify the aspects that support the creation of a lasting brand. The objective of this chapter is to outline the key principles that need to be focused on in the process of branding. This ensures a company stands out amidst the crowd and makes a positive impression on its consumers. You can achieve it by building an identity with the help of logos, symbols, messaging, colors that are bound to stay in trend in the long run. The success mantra to enhance brand recall is explained along with the quantity and style of writing and visual aesthetic that keeps consumers hooked. The chapter further dives into explaining the process of building an efficient brand strategy with the help of Keller's brand equity model and follows through into the four-step process of creating brand identity, brand meaning, brand response, and brand resonance. A significant measure of a successful brand strategy is understanding and defining brand sentiment, which can be derived from the values, voice, persona, brand positioning, and core messaging. Emphasizing the need to evoke an emotional connection with help of brand mission, brand promise, brand essence, and brand pillars helps reap a benefit that is far more superior to any profit in numbers as it can only be felt. After a thorough study on branding, the concept of brand marketing is tapped on to throw light onto the market execution strategies. The investment into branding can prove to be a game-changer and extend unlimited benefits for a brand's reputation leading to ever-increasing profits.

In marketing, I 've seen only one strategy that can 't miss — and that is to market to your best customers first, your best prospects second, and the rest of the world last.

—John Romero

Brand Process

Branding, as opposed to what everyone perceives it to be, is not a piece of cake. It is a tedious process involving proper logo making, slogan selections, and colors for an image to leave an ever-lasting impression on the target audience. Not giving enough attention to branding, you can lose out on attracting customers and potential partners and reduce the company's overall engagement with various stakeholders and the wider audience.
Stand out

PROCESS

DISCOVER	ANALYSE	DEFINE	CREATE	MANAGE
• History	• Company Goals	• Positioning	• Brand Name	• Launch
• Mission	• Target Audience	• Unique Selling	• Brand Slogan	Communication
• Culture and	• Brand	Proposition	• Logo	Kit
Value	Personality	• The Brand	• Visual Identity	• Brand
• Business	• Strength and	Distinct Voice	and Applications	Campaigns
Strategy	Weaknesses	• Brand Strategy	• Vision	• Guerilla
• Products and	• Opportunity and		• Brand Idea	Marketing
Services	threats		• Brand Unique	• Public Relations
• Direct	• Brand Attributes		Story	Support
Competitors	• Essential		• Brand	• Social Media
• The Market	Differentiators		Personality	Strategy
• Desk Research	• Market Trends		• Brand Rhetoric	• Events Concepts
• Interviews	• Internal		• Key-Messages	• Brand
• Branding	Resources		• Visual Style	Engagement
Questionnaire	• Key-people		• Graphic Platform	Sessions
• Customer			• Brand Guidelines	• Video
Satisfaction			• Retail Concept	• Apps & Mobile
• Digital Presence			Design	

Providing a differentiable and relevant product/service is critical to success. It stems from knowledge. As to who your competition is, who you are catering to, and what extraordinary you are giving to beat the competition and attract an audience.

The worst thing that could happen to a brand is to get mixed up with another one.

Sometimes, this happens unintentionally, but entrepreneurs intentionally copy popular brands to pry into their customer base. In the longer run, this is the worst idea. Copying branding trademarked by someone priorly can lead to expensive lawsuits. Even if it doesn't, copying someone's branding will definitely affect your reputation when you build one in the longer run.

Symbols that are here to stay

Sun Microsystems is a technology company owned by Oracle, specializing in developing innovative software and hardware. They have focused their branding on an image, and part of this image is about their logo; it features a bold red background and white lettering that stands above the crowd.

Stay in trend

Trends change fast, so great brands tend to choose more classic solutions for their logos, brand colors, inscriptions, and so on. Remember that classic doesn't mean boring—it means that designers should use more traditional fonts, shapes, colors, and imagery to stay popular for a more extended period.

Stay in mind

You name it, and the image should come simultaneously to the consumer's mind.

PCS—the mantra to remember
Personalize, Characterize, and Strategize

We can understand this mantra by the example of Comcast. By creating a logo that features a large red "C" around another C with black lettering in the rest of the brand name, the logo projects the idea of communications in an almost subliminal way.

A logo, perhaps one of the most important aspects of branding, was used by Comcast in a personalized and strategized way. Whether you know it or not, a business's logo is as essential as a brand's name.

Knowing your audience and capitalizing on how you can direct people to your services in a way that is a win–win situation for both parties. But, your logo serves as the way to do that. A method by which you must communicate value and worth to your intended audience.

The less, the better

Yes, if the maximum has to be achieved, minimalism is always the key.

Fewer colors: Let's look at some best-known brands; they splash their branding over with a massive set of vivid colorism. Also, they are seldom seen containing dozens of different lines and shapes. Logos made in online logo-makers, rewritten slogans, and a poor selection of colors don't take you a long way. Companies that don't give branding enough attention are not taken seriously, and they tend to have trouble attracting customers and business partners. The logo should be simple, easy to draw, and remember. The simple M of McDonald's will stay in your brain longer than anything else.

Fewer words: A brand slogan we know is useful, especially when it is short and easy to consumer's mind for a long time, and characterizes the brands it represents. Good slogans are timeless, and they can be repeatedly used in advertising. A perfect example is Netflix and Chill.

Stake your claim

Leading brands got where they are by marking their territory and capitalizing on it. A brand can do it in various ways by following a rigorous intellectual property rights (IPR) policy concerning branding designs, product patents, and so on. How do we know that a brand has reached the zenith of success? When its brand name is generic for its category, like Band-Aid, Google, Kleenex, or Xeroxor, its name has become synonymous with its unique character. Take, for instance, HEAD AND SHOULDERS. Anti-dandruff has become synonymous with its name. These brands have the same demarcated territory.

It's there; look closer

It is rightly said, don't make just customers for your products; make products for your customers.

Audi does a consumer-centric design and engineering; Audi ensures innovation tied to a driver's evolving needs. Its Tiptronic sedans l the driver's desire to avoid awkward gear changes with technology that provides the smoothest shifting among automobiles in its class. A brand can capitalize on a small idea and make it its pivotal branding point. That idea is right there. You can effortlessly just show it to the world.

The word of honor

A quality common to all significant brands of all times is the will to surpass consumer expectations, so you live up to your word. It not only leads to free word-of-mouth promotion but also creates widespread loyalty. Consumers know what to expect. They also know their money is safe where they put it. Companies like Apple are known for the product quality they provide. It gives what it says. Teamed with excellent customer service responsiveness, it can keep the word of honor it is known for.

Emotions matter

An emotional tie with customers guarantees immense potential. It is something that cannot be replicated by any other competitors of yours. They are unique and peculiar, induced in the audience by your brand and your brand only—emotions by creating a powerful connection with a consumer that anchors your brand in the consumer's psyche.

Harley–Davidson's counterculture emotions are what the brand has capitalized on. Do you think a consumer (rider) can feel the same way riding any other motorcycle? The answer is simply no.

Everything begins at home

A passionate band of employees can work as an effective mechanism for creating brand awareness. Firms that empower their workforce to carry out the brand promise to develop an intricate web of passionate brand advocates that carry out your word. These are the people who would be vocal about the good things you offer. Also, their word will be trusted the most. Moreover, they will be trusted most by the packed audience they cater to. The primary audience caters to the secondary, then the latter to tertiary, and the brand awareness web thus grows exponentially.

Own the means

Relying on your own media to carry out branding and marketing functions not only makes excellent financial sense, it also talks to customers more directly than any hired advertising can. This forms a unique area of influence that, of course, any competitor brand cannot tap.

Start a conversation

A restricted one-way flow of information from brand to consumer is dull and doesn't even serve the purpose. Today's brands are creating new avenues for two-way communication. The audience actively participates not just through online platforms and interactive experiences that help consumers bond with or influence the products and services they favor.

Advertisement is about creating discourse and then directing it to your advantage.

Branding should be and is increasingly becoming central to a consumer. It happens not in the physical world in consumers' minds and is an intangible resource with limitless potential yet to be tapped. Allegorically, the physical world is Plato's cave, and then when we leave that to enter consumers' minds, we have the ultimate reality. If we enter the consumer's mind, we would know the real picture of a brand.

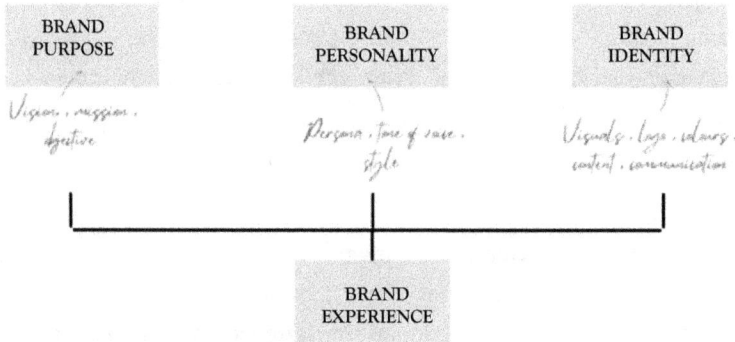

BRAND PURPOSE	BRAND PERSONALITY	BRAND IDENTITY
Vision . mission . objective	Persona . tone of voice . style	Visuals . logo . colours . content . communication

BRAND EXPERIENCE

Let us try to construct the underlying principles of branding. For this purpose, the process of branding can be split into three core components"

1. Brand strategy

Branding today is a multipronged exercise. It goes well beyond just a logo, a name, and basic ideas do not suffice. A full-fledged strategy is needed to make your message go across to the audience successfully.

Brands need a thorough understanding of why they choose specific strategies and a detailed outline of their plan. It is easy to understand why.

Because the more careful you are in your branding strategy, the easier it will be to succeed when executing those strategies.

Here are three definitional questions every brand needs to ask themselves.

- Who are you as a brand?
- Who are your customers?
- How does your brand define long-term success?

A brand strategy encompasses three basic tenets:

- What does your brand stand for?
- What promises your brand makes to customers?
- What personality your brand conveys through its communication and marketing?

As you can see, most of these considerations are abstractions. They are intangible. Now, how do you measure your success at getting through to the audience a specific brand personality? How do you identify and measure if you've successfully stood for what your brand represents or if something needs to be done?

Keller's brand equity model, first published in the book "Strategic Brand Management," also widely known as the customer-based brand equity (CBBE) model was pioneered by Professor Kevin Lane Keller, at the Tuck School of Business at Dartmouth College.

The premise of the brand equity model is simple: **to build a strong brand, one ought to groom how customers think and feel about one's product.** One needs to tailor the right type of experiences around the brand so that customers have virtuous thoughts, feelings, beliefs, opinions, and an overall optimistic outlook toward it.

Strong brand equity creates a lucrative loop of customers buying more of your product on their own, recommending it more often to others, breeding stronger loyalty, and hence, one is less likely to lose business to the competitors in the market.

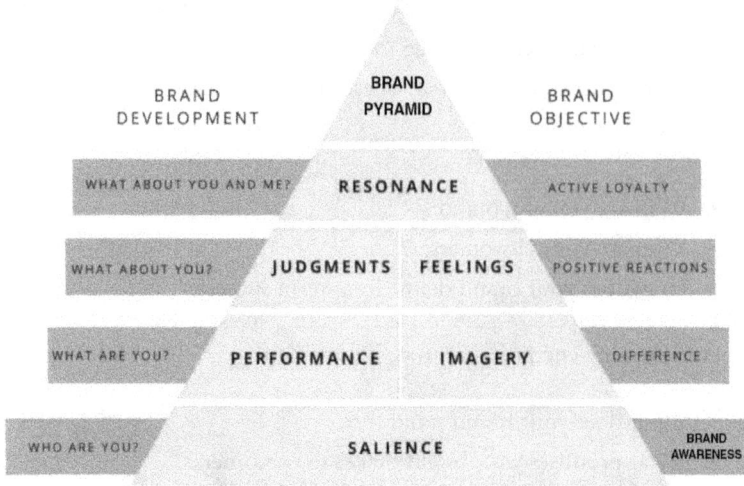

The model, seen in the preceding figure, illustrates the four steps needed to be followed to build strong brand equity. The four steps of the pyramid are representative of the four fundamental questions that your customers will ask—often subconsciously—about your brand.

The four steps contain six building blocks that must be in place for you to reach the top of the pyramid and be able to build a robust brand.

Let's look at each step and building block in detail and discuss how you can apply the framework and strengthen your brand better.

Step 1: Brand identity—Who are you?
The objective of the first step is to create "brand salience," or awareness—in uncomplicated words, you need to make sure that your brand stands out, and that customers recognize it and are aware of it.

You're not just not attempting to create brand identity and awareness here; you also have to ensure that brand perception is "correct" at the prime stages of the buying process.

Step 2: Brand meaning—What are you?
Your goal in Step 2 is to identify and enhance what your brand means and what it stands for. As simple as it sounds, both identification and communication of the same are arduous. However, a sound understanding of "performance" and "imagery" acts as two solid building blocks.

"Performance" is realized when your product meets your customers' needs. According to Keller, performance is composed of five tenets: primary characteristics and features; product reliability, durability, and serviceability; service effectiveness, efficiency, and empathy; style and design; and price.

"Imagery" suggests how well your brand meets your customers' needs on a social and psychological level. Your brand can meet these needs directly, from a customer's own experiences when using the product, or indirectly, with targeted marketing, or with word of mouth.

Step 3: Brand response—What do I think, or feel, about you?
"Judgments" and "feelings" are at the heart of what your customers' responses to what your brand is.

The customers consciously, as well as subconsciously, make judgments about your brand, and these fall into four key categories:

- Quality: The first judgment is reserved for the quality of a product by any consumer.
- Credibility: Customers judge credibility utilizing the trifecta of—expertise (which encompasses innovation), trustworthiness, and likability.
- Consideration: Customers estimate whether the product is relevant to suit their distinct needs.
- Superiority: Customers also engage in estimating what superior offerings your product promises compared to competitors' brands.

How the product makes the customers feel is a prime determinant of a customer's response to your brand. Feelings that are evoked directly is not the only exclusive way, but also includes the emotions of how a brand makes them feel about themselves. The model recognizes six positive brand feelings: warmth, excitement, security, fun, social approval, and self-respect.

Step 4: Brand resonance—How much of a connection would I like to have with you?

Brand "resonance" is the zenith of the brand equity pyramid because it is the most grueling—and the most desirable—level to reach. You have achieved brand resonance when your customers have a deep-seated psychological bond with your brand.

Keller breaks resonance down into four categories:

- **Behavioral loyalty:** This includes repeated purchases despite the availability of other options in the market.
- **Attitudinal attachment:** Your customers feel a higher intensity of fondness for your brand, and they view it as something that is beyond the quotidian purchase.
- **Sense of community:** Your customers feel a sense of community with people associated with the brand, including other consumers and company representatives.
- **Active engagement:** This is the ultimate level of brand loyalty. When customers are actively engaged with your brand, even when they are not actively purchasing or consuming it presently. This can take the form of joining a club related to the brand; participating in online chats, marketing rallies, or events; following your brand on social media; or taking part in other such activities.

A significant measure of a successful brand strategy is understanding and defining brand sentiment. Although it is hard to measure, it doesn't mean it should stop you from trying to measure it. It may be difficult to quantify. Hence, even analytical Chief Executive Officers (CEOs) tend to dismiss the qualitative work involved in branding, which is irreplaceable to gauge success—even Airbnb CEO Brian Chesky made so clear:

> The designing of experience is a different part of your brain than the scaling [of] your experience. It's a different skill set. The scaling experience is a highly analytical, operations-oriented, and technology-oriented problem. The designing of experience is a more intuition-based human, empathetic, end-to-end experience.

The essential steps involved in this process are laid out as follows.

Values—what you believe in

For many businesses, brand values act as the "true north" on their compass toward market success. Regardless of how you might go on your branding journey, your core brand values will remain fixed and steady. This means that while the logo, products, website, and even the digital marketing campaigns may change, your brand values must always remain constant.

Values of your brand define how it works, what principles drive it, and a rough boundary that encapsulates the branding actions.

Voice—how do you sound

Tone-deaf marketing has hurt many a brand beyond repair. To have a voice is to find the correct tone for your brand.

To find the right tone for your brand, you need to know your audience and consider their taste and sensitivity. You also need to understand how your message sounds to them.

To find your brand voice, start by asking yourself these three questions:

1. Who am I writing this piece for?
2. What am I trying to tell my audience?
3. How do I want my audience to feel?

Persona—how do you act

A brand persona encompasses personality traits, attitudes, and core values of your back, basically your brand face, which helps it connect with the audience, somewhat visible to the audience. A brand persona can be a person, character, mascot, just an idea. Whatever of these encapsulates the representation. Your company needs a face that is uncontestable.

Certain benefits are going to arise out of a brand persona are:

1. It might nudge your brand to put in the necessary effort, which it might otherwise tend to put off
2. Your brand will go through essential soul searching because of it

Brand positioning—where do you stand
Brand positioning has been defined by Kotler as "the act of designing the company's offering and image to occupy a distinctive place in the mind of the target market." In other words, brand positioning outlines how your brand sits in customers' minds. Brand positioning strategies are linked to consumer/customer's loyalty toward the brand, brand equity (consumer-based), and the customer's will to purchase from the brand. Basically, brand positioning stands for shaping consumer preferences, which a firm can easily do for its own advantage.

Core message—what are you able to convey
Every excellent brand world its brand name carries a core brand message compact statement that declares why the brand matters, what it stands for, and how it stands apart from competitors. Brand messaging is never given as much importance, yet it plays a pivotal role in the process. Through a core message, a brand displays the human side of its efforts. A human side resonates with a customer's minds mind, creating an understanding that is more than just an absolute value addition.

The benefit it ushers is beyond numbers and metrics. It's a feeling.

1. Brand mission
2. Brand promise
3. Brand essence
4. Brand pillars

These abstractions are components of and further translate into the **brand identity.**

An effective branding process results in a unique identity that differentiates you from the competition and can be the heart of a competitive strategy.

Developing a brand strategy can be one of the most challenging steps in your overall marketing plan. Still, it is essential because it is the pivot of your brand identity and is communicated consistently in myriad ways throughout your business. The fact that it makes a difference is ubiquitous and should be common knowledge.

2. Brand identity

Brand identity is a recognizable brand and visible to an audience, including color, design, and a brand's logo. It's how a business presents itself to the audience and distinguishes the company in consumers' minds. Put simply: brand identity is what you can see in your brand.

Brand identity consists of various elements, including:

- Logo or wordmark
- Different logo variations
- Key brand colors and color palette
- Typefaces
- Typographic treatments
- A consistent style for images and content
- Library of graphical elements
- Style guide
- Your visual identity on social media

3. Brand marketing

A company's brand also represents its market identity, which includes abstract things like trustworthiness, quality expectations, promise delivery, customer support expectations, and so on.

Effective brand marketing mandates the capabilities of a brand to communicate a clear and compelling message. It additionally consists of the ability to collect and analyze data that supports your marketing message. That is précising why there is a need for developing marketing degree programs. These processes are complex and intricately woven together with a unique marketing communication that is very important for your business to function par excellence.

What is marketing communication?

Marketing communication refers to all such activities and initiatives undertaken by brand managers to build and maintain the brand image among the targeted customers (Duncan and Mulhern 2004). It is a strategic decision that drives competitive advantage to attract, retain, and leverage customers (Kitchen, Joanne and Tao 2004). Duncan (2002) explained that marketing communication is a fundamental process for managing the customer relationship that makes brand value last. Marketing communication programs not only include above-the-line activities such as advertising and sales promotions but also below-the-line activities, for instance, public relations. Recent concepts of marketing communication, two-way as well as one-way communication both are considered a key determinant of brand strategies to stimulate the brand orientation process (Aaker 1996 and Urde 1994).

The Differences Between Brand Building and Marketing Activation

Brand Building	Marketing Activation
Creates Mental Brand Equity	Exploits Mental Brand Equity
Influences Future Sales	Generates Sales Now
Broad Reach	Tightly Targeted
Long term	Short Term
Emotional Priming	Persuasive Messages

Branding should be and is increasingly becoming central to a consumer. It happens not in the physical world in consumers' minds and is an intangible resource with limitless potential yet to be tapped. Allegorically, the physical world is Plato's cave, and then when we leave that to enter consumers' minds, we have the ultimate reality. If we enter the consumer's mind, we would know the real picture of a brand. The process can end in itself; if care is taken, the benefits from this process are limitless. Branding should be understood as an art that understands the opportunity cost to an optimal cost–benefit analysis. Investing in branding is investing in goodwill beyond just profit margins. Brands and entrepreneurs will continue to find branding the game-changer.

Key Takeaways

1. *Providing a differentiable and relevant product/service is critical to success. It stems from knowledge. As to who your competition is, who you are catering to, and what extraordinary you are giving to beat the competition and attract an audience.*

2. *A passionate band of employees can work as an effective mechanism for creating brand awareness. Firms that empower their workforce to carry out the brand promise to develop an intricate web of passionate brand advocates that carry out your word.*

3. *Branding today is a multipronged exercise. It goes well beyond just a logo, a name, and basic ideas do not suffice. A full-fledged strategy is needed to make your message go across to the audience successfully.*

4. *The premise of Keller's brand equity model, is simple: to build a strong brand, one ought to groom how customers think and feel about one's product. One needs to tailor the right type of experiences around the brand so that customers have virtuous thoughts, feelings, beliefs, opinions, and an overall optimistic outlook toward it.*

5. *You're not just not attempting to create brand identity and awareness here; you also have to ensure that brand perception is "correct" at the prime stages of the buying process.*

6. *Your goal in step two is to identify and enhance what your brand means and what it stands for.*

7. *The customers consciously, as well as subconsciously, make judgments about your brand, and these fall into four key categories: quality, credibility, consideration, superiority.*

8. *You have achieved brand resonance when your customers have a deep-seated psychological bond with your brand.*

9. *Values of your brand define how it works, what principles drive it, and a rough boundary that encapsulates the branding actions.*

10. *A brand persona is/are personality traits, attitudes, and core values of your back, basically your brand face, which helps it connect with the audience, somewhat visible to the audience.*

11. *Brand positioning has been defined by Kotler as "the act of designing the company's offering and image to occupy a distinctive place in the mind of the target market." In other words, brand positioning outlines how your brand sits in customers' minds.*

12. *Brand identity is a recognizable brand and visible to an audience, including color, design, and a brand's logo.*

13. *Effective brand marketing mandates the capabilities of a brand to communicate a clear and compelling message. It additionally consists of the ability to collect and analyze data that supports your marketing message.*

Brand Process

Step 1: *Discover the purpose and reason for your brand's existence.*
Why do you exist?
How are you different?
What are you offering?

Step 2: *Research your direct completion or benchmark brands.*
Assign a score to each and list down the following:
Messaging and visual identity
Products or services
Customer reviews or social mentions
Market their business—online and offline

Step 3: *Detail persona, behavior, and lifestyle of your target audience.*
Describe the following:
Age
Gender
Location
Income
Education level
Motivations
Goals
Pain points
Influencers
Brand affinities

Step 4: *Create a mission statement.*
Mission statement = Why + What + How + Who
Your brand identity—the logo, tagline, voice, messaging, and personality should reflect this mission.
Example
Nike: *"To bring inspiration and innovation to every athlete in the world."*
JetBlue: *"To inspire humanity — both in the air and on the ground."*
Tesla: *"To accelerate the world's transition to sustainable energy."*
TED: *"Spread ideas."*

LinkedIn: *"To connect the world's professionals to make them more productive and successful."*
PayPal: *"To build the web's most convenient, secure, cost-effective payment solution."*
Amazon: *"To be Earth's most customer-centric company, where customers can find and discover anything they might want to buy online, and endeavors to offer its customers the lowest possible prices."*

Step 5: *List down your unique selling proposition.*
Emotional benefit
Functional benefit
Experience benefit
Market benefit
Product features
Example
Apple doesn't sell electronics, it sells—smart choice, ease of use, creativity, innovation, clean design

Step 6: *Identify your brand's tone of voice.*
TOV is developed from your brand's mission, target audience, and sector. This is how you speak to your customers.

Pick only three from the list:

1. *Authoritative*
2. *Caring*
3. *Cheerful*
4. *Coarse*
5. *Conservative*
6. *Conversational*
7. *Casual*
8. *Dry*
9. *Edgy*
10. *Enthusiastic*
11. *Formal*
12. *Frank*

13. *Friendly*

14. *Fun*

15. *Funny*

16. *Humorous*

17. *Informative*

18. *Irreverent*

19. *Matter of fact*

20. *Nostalgic*

21. *Passionate*

22. *Playful*

23. *Professional*

24. *Provocative*

25. *Quirky*

26. *Respectful*

27. *Romantic*

28. *Sarcastic*

29. *Serious*

30. *Smart*

31. *Snarky*

32. *Sympathetic*

33. *Trendy*

34. *Trustworthy*

35. *Unapologetic*

36. *Upbeat*

37. *Witty*

Step 7: *Define your brand persona.*
This is why, people connect with you, it's your personality. It's how you act.

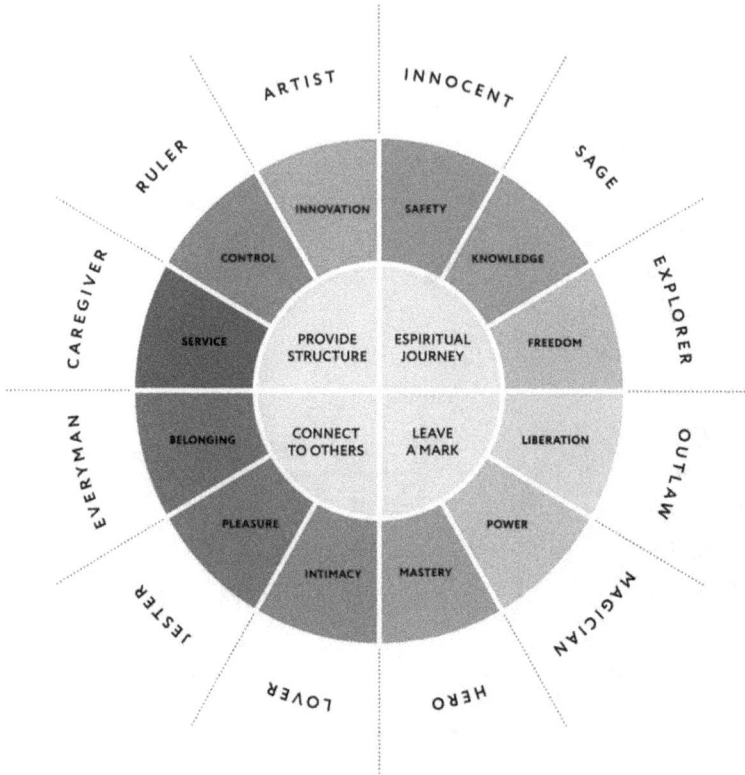

Are you :
Personable or corporate
Friendly or professional
Spontaneous or planner
Energetic or laid-back
Modern or classic
Updated or traditional
New or established
Forward-thinking or conservative
What motivates you?
Belongingness = Social
Risk achievement = Ego

Learning = Freedom
Stability = Order
This persona is why people connect with you, it's your personality. It's how you act.

Step 8: Create your brand positioning in the market.
Why will people come to you?
What do you want them to think about you?
What is your standing in the industry?

Step 9: Create your core message and story.
Who you are?
What you offer?
Why do you matter?
Through a core message, a brand displays the human side of its efforts.

Step 10: List down your brand pyramid (Keller pyramid)

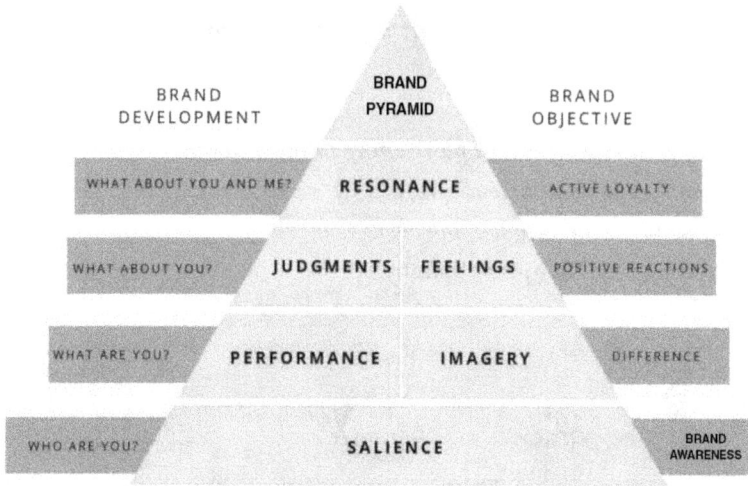

Example: Red Bull

This translated into all your designs, copy, text, visuals, and execution.

Step 11: Design your brand identity.

It consists of tangible and recognizable elements that stay consistent for the brand's recall value:

Name

Tagline

Imagery

Iconography

Visual language

Logo—with usage guidelines

Colors—with exact color codes

Typography—with fonts, sizes, and its usage

Step 12: Identify marketing channels.

Effective brand marketing mandates the capabilities of a brand to communicate a clear and compelling message to its audience by using the right platform.

Online/offline

ATL/BTL

Organic/paid

CHAPTER 6

Overview

Brand champions showcases real-life applications of what has been explained in the previous chapters. This is done by introducing the reader to some of the best-branded companies and the best strategies in history so far. Good branding combines subject-matter competence with the customer experience and a curated social media presence. Good storytelling has been described to be the essence of good marketing. The companies that have been discussed in this chapter have nailed the concepts like brand positioning, brand drifting, and the effects of harnessing the power of emotions.

Brand positioning is how a brand is perceived differently from the competitors and how consumers relate to and connect with a brand. Brand Drift created a concept of "Conversational Marketing" and built a tool focusing on a new marketing aspect. For instance, Tesla's branding makes sure that its high price is never the problem; as it mainly focuses on quality. Companies like Starbucks, P&G, Simmons, and more have all sustained their brand awareness, lead generation, and engagement with meaningful, appealing content that is in line with their business values. Post discussing the success of these brands, the key learnings are exemplified, which include building strong trust and building interactive relationships with consumers over social media can advocate the presence of the human element, in return encouraging brand loyalty. Many brands have outperformed others by advocating "Conscious Branding," which harnesses the vision and purpose of a company that supports positivity with long-term growth and mindful steps to serve the well-being of people and the planet.

Brand Champions

A brand is a voice, and a product is a souvenir.

—Lisa Gransky

Good branding combines subject-matter competence with the customer experience and a curated social media presence. It would be fit if you spotted the mantra that each action you take is to charm your customers and encourage them to keep coming back to you. Brand positioning is how a brand is perceived differently from the competitors and how consumers relate to and connect with a brand.

Brand Drift created a concept of **"Conversational Marketing"** and built a tool focusing on a new marketing aspect. Ideas' two-way exchange is emphasized in this unique kind of marketing rather than unidirectional conversational production and consumption. This approach is one of many models of marketing that has worked wonders.

Conversational Marketing

Context Personal touch Real time

Even hilarious, engaging, and creative campaigns are alternative models that have had enormous success. Carlsberg's honest, light-hearted campaign in 2019 showed just this. **Carlsberg** advertised its lager as "Probably the best beer in the world" for almost 40 years of being in the market. Customers started disagreeing. Carlsberg made a smart move by starting an afresh campaign, *probably not*. Is Carlsberg the best beer? Probably not. It was fun, and the virtue of newfound credibility was the icing on the cake.

Tesla cars are state-of-the-art luxury vehicles, being long-range, eco-friendly, and electric is the cherry on the cake. But, these cars are costly. Tesla's branding makes sure that is never the problem; its branding focuses on quality. Don't like it, return it within seven days for a full refund.

Branding Harnesses the Power of Emotions

Humans are emotional creatures, fond of ideas, stories, and even products that touch their hearts, inducing emotions. Also, emotions always win over logic when it comes to developing brand loyalty.

Take, for instance, the ads shown during the **2016 Rio Olympics.** The several popular ads were the ones that combined emotions and experiences to create an emotional connection with the audience.

Also, **PG&E's** "Thank you Mom" advertisement showed key themes emerging out of unique anecdotes from the lives of athletes whose mothers shielded them from fatal situations so that they could be the most robust version of themselves. The emotion of a mother's protective care was portrayed beautifully and harnessing its power to make connections.

Branding displays a method of creating an emotional statement every time your customers come across your product or service or something that reminds them about it—through engaging storytelling—which engages your audience's subconscious mind and builds an emotional bridge between the story and the brand.

The human side of branding will always remain universally relevant, mainly when all we have is a few milliseconds to engage with our audiences emotionally.

Give your customers a good enough reason to care about your brand. This value is how customers transition from being fence-sitters to active participants and, as a result, come closer to buying your product. Years of research tell us it is emotions and not logic that drives most buyers' purchase decisions.

The Case of Conscious Branding

Simmons & Co.

It is one of the central investment banks in the energy industry. In a case study by Simmons & Co., where the company's marketing plan was analyzed and sought to be improved. They realized a need for a better connection to the people they catered to. Hence, they conducted numerous surveys and interviewed the consumers of their services, looking for possible improvements. They came out with a new avatar of branding, which incorporated the ideas of their customers. Of course, this worked wonders with branding as it could cover the scope and objective of their services in a holistic manner.

The Case of Honest Branding

Ford

Sometimes, we learn best from our mistakes. When Ford made an error that involved threatening lawsuits for copyright infringement, Ford immediately informed the public about the error online. They used social media for "damage control" or instead save itself, and its swift response helped regain their fan base. It is essential to react immediately when negative comments or statements appear on social media platforms. Maintaining your brand's integrity is mostly determined by your ability to correct mistakes quickly if you make mistakes that are prone to be interpreted negatively. This engagement will help a quick bounce back from all potential damage inflicted by social media comments and interpretations that may be put out.

Nike won the big brand winner title at the women's World Cup when their ad "Dream Further" showcased female footballers' talent across the world—without any clichéd message that comes with other female-empowerment ads. Nike's "Don't change your dreams. Change the world" is an inspiring, emotional, and authentic celebration of female athletes. As always in this ad, too, Nike's referencing to the brand was subtle and never deflecting from the greater narrative. Such connotative branding works much better than the emphatic one and can be considered an excellent way to go.

What Can We Learn From This?

When creating a narrative on social media campaigns, it is important to stay authentic and genuine, or at least appear so. Trust is essential, and people trust people, more manageable than brands or mere abstract ideas, so make sure your social media content sounds like it has a real human voice. Nike does well in engaging with human nature through all its platforms, online or offline.

Effective social media content should always show your prospects that you understand their wants and ground reality. It is an opportunity to showcase your product/service. Content should have value and a purpose. Its brand awareness, lead generation, or engagement building—content should be meaningful, appealing, and in line with why your business provides your product or service.

Festivals witness the most high-spirited branding. Taking, for example, Christmas Hafod Hardware's came up with a £100 advert that rivaled other big-budget ads such as that of John Lewis (a much bigger brand). This small independent family-run hardware store stole the hearts of the U.S.'s people and grabbed the attention of the world when their advertisement "Be a kid this Christmas" went viral on YouTube. The ad shows the traditional Christmas spirit and the importance of community. While they do borrow storyline tropes from companies like John Lewis, it's all about execution—which Hafod Hardware managed to do very well.

Some cases to ponder upon

There is nothing black and white, especially in business. Here are some cases where brands stand confused as to which direction to move in. Let this dilemma be food for thought.

The case describes the ugly truth that cocoa production in the Côte d'Ivoire involved child slave labor. These controversial stories affected Cadbury, especially hard. Cadbury's brand culture had been deeply rooted in its founders' religious traditions, and the organization had paid close attention to its workers' goodwill and sourcing practices. The U.S. Congress was considering legislation that can acknowledge chocolate grown on certified plantations labeled "slave labor free," placing the rest of the industry in a bad light. Chocolate producers had asked for time to rectify the situation, but the extension they negotiated was running out.

Here I ask you to contemplate if Cadbury should associate with the industry to lobby for more time? What else could Cadbury do to make sure that its supply chain was ethically run? What should a good brand strategy for Cadbury be?

Let us look at SELCO, India's innovative solar electric company that sought to bring solar electric appliances to the poor. In 2009, the company was looking for a new growth strategy. The company's dilemma is whether it should go "deeper" and serve even more imperfect people or go "wider" and expand beyond its current geographical areas. In doing so, how is the image of the brand affected?

SELCO was at a strategic crossroads; what would a good branding strategy here be?

Good work is its mouthpiece. Doing a larger good for society creates more significant goodwill. In both, the aforementioned dilemmas both ways seem good to go, but one way is nearly right. In the first case, a seemingly ethical step would save the company from being abashed, and in the second case, an honest effort of serving the poor would create good publicity.

To produce an excellent social media campaign or an advertising campaign, for that matter, you don't need a huge budget. At the same time, it's great if you have considerable money reserved for it. But, we should appreciate that companies can achieve much more from an authentic, thoughtful, and relatable campaign. One should keep in mind the buyer's persona, and it is essential to think as to what content will resonate with them the most—be thought-provoking and engaging. Regardless of the industry, knowing your customers always helps; by doing this, you'll be able to sell your product or service to them much more effectively.

Key Takeaways

1. *As Lisa Gransky suggests, the product you finally sell is like a gift for your consumers, which is advocated and advertised by utilizing branding as its voice.*

2. *To create a good brand, it is essential to have expertise in your industry, provide seamless customer experiences, and stay in touch with them through social media platforms.*

3. *How well your consumers can stay connected and hooked onto coming back to your brand depends on the positioning and authenticity in contrast to other competitors.*

4. *Conversational marketing encourages bilateral conversation with consumers in the process of creation-consumption and has made a positive impact on user retention.*

5. *Carlsberg played a smart move by utilizing humor as a means of advertisement to avoid controversy and lighten up the brand image, which helped it build fun and credible reputation.*

6. *Although Tesla is extremely expensive and falls under the luxury segment, its reputation for building strong and environmentally friendly cars overshadow the high price factor. They boast their high quality by topping off their purchases with a seven-day full refund policy.*

7. *As emotional beings, humans enjoy associating with brands that touch their hearts through unique ideas, innovation, and especially stories. Most consumers are even willing to accommodate pricing changes if they feel connected with certain brands/products.*

8. *Years of research tell us it is emotions and not logic that drives most buyers' purchase decisions.*

9. *The Rio Olympics 2016 is an exceptional example of utilizing emotions in advertising to impact consumers' minds.*

10. *PG&E's "Thank you, Mom" advertisement showed the emotion of a mother's protective care, which was portrayed beautifully and harnessing its power to make connections.*

11. *You have only a very minute period to connect with your audience, so be sure to make high efforts to create awareness about the value your products or services add to their lives.*

12. *Many brands have outperformed others by advocating "Conscious Branding," which harnesses the vision and purpose of a company that supports positivity with long-term growth and mindful steps to serve the well-being of people and the planet.*

13. *Simmons & Co. made efforts to conduct thorough research on their consumers' needs and desired services and took the challenge of making holistic improvements for enhanced experiences.*

14. *Honesty is considered one of the lowest virtues among large businesses, and it is still highly valued by consumers. In this case, Ford was applauded for its humble behavior and apologizing for an error that turned into a public relations (PR) nightmare. The company's effort to maintain its integrity upheld its reputation in a resilient fashion.*

15. *As connotative branding makes for a good impression, Nike's "Don't change your dreams. Change the world" is an inspiring, emotional, and authentic celebration of female athletes, winning the Big Brand Winner title at the women's World Cup.*

16. *Social media is a place where you have the opportunity to showcase your valued product/service, showing your prospects that you understand their desires. Utilize meaningful and appealing content apt for your business.*

17. *Festive season appears to be the most rewarding season, which is why Hafod Hardware had heads turning to their viral video initiative portraying the importance of community and harmony.*

18. *With growing awareness across the globe, it isn't easy to increase profits without addressing consumers, producers, or workers' fundamental rights. Controversies can cripple any brand's goodwill as reality, and the implications of their brand may be contradictory.*

19. *Cadbury's case of child labor was an attack on its intrinsic ethical, cultural values, religious traditions, attention to its workers' goodwill, and sourcing practices.*

20. *Often, brands can be found at crossroads, much like SELCO, where it had to make the tough decision of growing geographically or socially. Corporate social responsibility (CSR) is considered a large factor in creating more substantial goodwill, which certainly supports greater profits in the long term.*

21. *Keep in mind that spending excessive amounts of advertising resources is not always directly proportional to the ROI. Hence, the lack of large budgets must not demean social media efforts, if done smartly.*

CHAPTER 7

Overview

In continuation to case studies of famous brand strategies, "Guilty Brands" throws light on some of the brands that contributed to the list of the most infamous and failed strategies. Ranging from ad campaigns of Gillette portraying toxic masculinity to Iceland to Ancestry depicting slavery, to Cadbury being found guilty of child labor, and more. The negative effect that these campaigns had on the reputation of some of the world's largest companies is speculated in detail. The thought of social consequences when ignored in the portrayals of marketing ventures could do more harm than good. Magnifying the point that sometimes trying to make an impact can lose direction, and even the idea of focusing on social causes can backfire, if not executed sensitively. Noting that 91 percent of the consumers agree that they would buy from brands that support a good cause, which makes it essential for companies to ensure not just their branding, but even their company values and processes are clean from any unethical practices. The chapter outlines that regardless of industry one caters to while creating a brand image, it must be remembered that good publicity goes a long way, but there is nothing worse than bad publicity.

Guilty Brands

It takes 20 years to build a reputation and five minutes to ruin it. If you think about that, you'll do things differently.

—Warren Buffett

Ad campaigns range from **Gillette** portraying toxic masculinity to **Iceland**, raising awareness for deforestation focusing on social and environmental issues; this is social responsibility marketing. This kind of marketing is high on trends these days. And, why shouldn't it be? In a global survey, **a whopping 91 percent of the customers** reported that they were likely to buy from a brand that supports a good cause. It is contestable if they would actually make the purchase, but if they do, consumers expect to receive the same quality and price from the brand.

Does social responsibility marketing always pay off? The answer is a simple no. It might face backlash; it might meet appreciation, but is it the only way? Of course, not. But, thinking it the other way around when in your branding, you forget to think about the social consequences of the portrayals that your marketing ventures encapsulate, your branding could do more harm than good.

To understand this, let's take a peek into

Cases Where Audience Found a Major Fault With Branding.

Here are some of the underlying accusations.

Guilty of Racism

A famous clothing brand, H&M, once posted an image on its website of an African-American child modeling a green sweatshirt that said the slogan "Coolest Monkey in the Jungle." The audience worldwide was outraged at the cultural insensitivity, which was perceived to be containing racial innuendos.

Guilty of Romanticizing Slavery

A YouTube campaign by an American brand Ancestry created a massive uproar in its audience when its ad featured a white man asking a black woman to leave town with him. The narrative of the ad set in 1850 brought about bitter memories of slavery, violence, and oppression. This concept was done to encourage people to get a DNA test to discover their family heritage. The entire purpose was defeated. The message couldn't have gone more wrong.

Guilty of Colorism

Cosmetic brand Estee Lauder, in its new line of foundation, released over 30 shades. With only a couple of darker shades, most of the foundation's shades catered to women with ashen, pale, or very fair skin tones. This limited vision of reality was perceived as brand arrogance because it was seen that the foundation was catering to only the specific complexion customers.

Guilty of Ethnic Stereotyping

Advertisement for the company showcases a Chinese model attempting—and failing—to eat different Italian dishes with chopsticks. The ad was perceived to be portraying Chinese women as lacking poise cultural sensitivity. The hashtag #BoycottDolce began trending on the Chinese social media site Weibo. They were also compelled to cancel their Shanghai runway show, which made them lose millions.

D&G
DOLCE & GABBANA

Guilty of Unsustainability

Climate change and environmental sustainability of consumer goods have been the new century's discourse, especially with youngsters. Research shows that up to 80 percent of the "millennials" worldwide, especially Australia, Canada, China, India, the UK, and the United States, find it essential for businesses to cut down their environmental impact.

So, fast-fashion is something they are bound to find faults with. When a company, **Misguided**, announced the launch of a £1 bikini on Instagram, despite the product selling out, the immediate outcry of the Misguided campaign caused by the young audience of Instagram hurt the company's image a great deal. Just profit will not suffice your branding need, definitely not in the longer run.

Profit is the necessary aim of your branding but not a sufficient condition.

Guilty of Faking it

Consumers are sensitive to manipulation. It is never wise for you to presume that they will not notice discrepancies in marketing. Cause marketing campaigns that are misguided invited backlash in a recent campaign by Pepsi featuring supermodel Kendell Jenner where she cancels police brutality with a mere can of Pepsi. In the climate of "Black Lives Matter" protest, this was seen as a ridiculous attempt of hijacking the narrative to cash in on the turmoil. The ad couldn't even stand 24 hours in the public domain. Additionally, it ushered terrible taste in the larger audience, not to mention the public apology the brand had to give.

There are various other ways a brand can get its marketing wrong.

Worst of all, ignorance

Adidas launched a Twitter campaign to promote a new partnership with Arsenal football club. Hoping the Adidas Twitter account followers would tweet with the hashtag #DareToCreate and, in doing so, send an automated response featuring an image of users' handles printed on the back of an Arsenal shirt.

The automatic reply function became the "Achilles heel" of this seemingly powerful campaign, which left it vulnerable to abuse by Twitter trolls. Extremely offensive handles were submitted. Apparent ignorance of the loopholes in an automated hashtag campaign, Adidas stands guilty of lousy marketing. A business should be aware of the danger automation entails.

Saving face—miscalculated marketing

A Russian Domino's franchise outlet released a campaign, "Dominos Forever," which offered 100 free pizzas a year for the next 100 years to customers who get the brand's logo tattooed on their body. Sounds great, right? When Dominos found out that they had gravely miscalculated the number of die-hard pizza lovers and underestimated their love for pizza, the idea didn't look great. After hundreds of inked social media posts poured in Dominos, to save face, new conditions like the size of the tattoo, 350-person cap on the offer, all retrospectively. Dominos eventually had to pull back its request short of time.

A misanthropic philanthropy
MasterCard proposed to donate 10,000 meals to developing countries for every goal scored by Messi or Neymar Jr in the FIFA 2018 tournament. The idea was outrageous; brows were raised at the intentions of the brand. It was suggested to either drop this idea insulting to the starving altogether or donate irrespective of any silly goal count. The company abashed by the public shaming had to concede to the demands. The entire venture was a lost cause.

Key lessons to learn here
No matter what business you are in, you will benefit a great deal from paying attention to the conversations they're having. The discourse is

creating your brand image—wanting publicity should always realize that there is such a thing as bad publicity. Whatever you do in your branding venture, do not go against the larger ethical and value systems.

These social media blunders can teach businesses how not to advertise and generate content. It's essential to keep the audience sentiments at the forefront of content creation, irrespective of your business. Never lose sight of what it is you're trying to achieve here with the narrative you peddle. Instead of upsetting your customers with tone-deaf messaging, give them what they deserve, what they can easily relate to.

Automation or steal deals or thrifty products are cheap marketing; it can be great; it saves time and effort. However, social media is a perilous space prone to be misused. These double-edged swords of marketing should be used absolutely in a sparing way.

Convenient automation such as auto-reply, chatbots, and many more is promising but effective only with constant monitoring.

Social media is Pandora's box—*"A source of great and unexpected troubles"* that has to be opened but with the expectation of the unexpected. It can be detrimental for your business, as can it be advantageous. Using all of this wisely and effectively to your advantage is an art. An art that is not known to everybody in the business, and that's what makes all the difference.

Key Takeaways

1. *Warren Buffet makes a real statement by mentioning that it takes a long time to build goodwill for any brand and just a fraction of it to ruin it. Everyone must have this in the back of their heads while making any strategic decisions for their companies.*

2. *Corporate social responsibility is not something to be followed in social actions and marketing campaigns, as today's consumers are inclined to buy from socially conscious brands over those that are not.*

3. *Though socially responsible marketing may appear to be a great option, the returns may or may not directly reflect profits. If not executed appropriately, it, in fact, causes more harm than benefits, leading to accusations like racism, romanticizing flawed norms, unsustainability, or even putting up facades.*

4. *H&M faced a harsh response by posting an Afro-American model in its attempt to be humorous and was tagged for being racist and culturally insensitive.*

5. *Ancestry is proof of an advertising stunt gone entirely wrong, as it outraged a massive audience through its YouTube campaign where it was perceived to romanticize slavery!*

6. *Estee Lauder failed miserably to create more color options for women as it introduced a more extensive range of foundations for light skin tones versus its claim to cater to "all" complexions.*

7. *Direct targeting and ethnic stereotyping is a big NO, which is sure to gain big lousy PR and possible remarks like #BoycottDolce when the brand portrayed the Chinese woman incapable of growing accustomed to western etiquette.*

8. *Heavily affected by current environmental changes, 80 percent of the millennials that make up the largest segment of the market in the present time do not take unsustainability as an option from companies they buy from. Fast-fashion and cheap sellouts are sure not to leave a positive impression on their minds.*

9. *No matter what, misguided advertising or manipulation of facts can crush an age-old brand's worth in a minute. Likewise was Pepsi's case, where it tried to nullify the effects of forced brutality with a can of their beverage offered by a supermodel.*

10. *Ignorance of the loopholes in an automated hashtag campaign, Adidas stands guilty of lousy marketing. A business should be aware of the danger automation entails.*

11. *Companies must do proper research before launching potentially miscalculated marketing, a disaster that Domino's put itself through in Russia. Underestimating the number of pizza lovers that did not consider getting the brand tattooed on them really fired back.*

12. *The fine print "terms and conditions" is never taken too well. Especially if it involves any forms of misanthropy, one can be sure to find their efforts hitting rock bottom like MasterCard. Their philanthropic move of donating thousands of meals based on the number of goals made by a few players made the entire idea appear very fake and brought the company into an extreme lousy light.*

13. *Regardless of your business or industry, you will benefit by not going against the larger ethical and value systems.*

14. *It's essential to keep the audience sentiments at the forefront of content creation, irrespective of your business.*

15. *Instead of upsetting your customers with tone-deaf messaging, give them what they deserve, what they can easily relate to.*

16. *Convenient automation such as auto-reply, chatbots, and many more is promising but effective only with constant monitoring.*

CHAPTER 8

Overview

Consumer buying behavior involves their decision-making prowess that is stimulated by sensory messaging in the form of sight, sounds, smell, taste, and stories. A brand signifies a connection other than what is derived from its tangible product/services. This chapter aims to simplify the understanding of how branding affects perception and the potential it has to amplify the overall brand experience. Extensive research on the behavior of consumers is showcased whereby culture and social status are presented as examples of major factors that influence consumer buying behavior. Upon zooming out, the variants of buying behaviors are easily recognizable based on the product or service. Complex buying behavior, habitual buying behavior, and variety-seeking buying behavior are defined, followed by Howard's three-category consumer decision-making theory of (i) routine response programmed behavior, (ii) limited decision making, and (iii) extensive decision making. Herbert's dissonance-reducing buyer behavior is also discussed in detail, followed by an understanding of the steps in the buying decision process. The chapter continues to explore the possibilities of gauging the opportunities to serve consumers through making efforts to understand their psychology. Statistics and examples from studies showcase that social media and word of mouth are the most effective methods of growing and improving brand image. Ending with a note and short exercise on the importance of having a clear buyer persona helps any brand with the information needed to harness the power of social, word of mouth, and influencers to boost positive brand perception. Through the given exercise, the reader can expect to learn about additional benefits from quality, availability, identification, mind-share branding, cultural branding, emotional branding, viral branding, sensory branding.

Affecting Perception

A brand goes well past the offering of a tangible product. It is more than just the sum of its products. It has its personality representing a company's very soul, including its vision, mission, or culture. So, it is not hard to appreciate that the brand as a personality resonates with customers personally as a mental impression or perception. Customer mind processes, like other experiences, would feel sensory messages. Hence, a brand can create a unique perception, and marketing should take full advantage of the phenomenon by exposing it to all our senses:

Sight: Instantly recognizable logos (Dominos, Coca-Cola, McDonald's, Disney (Mickey Mouse logo), Cadbury, PG Tips) and high-budget, entertaining commercials, giant billboards everywhere. Display windows of brand outlets, appetizing food photography, fancy product photography.

Sound: Catchy musical jingles (Intel) or catchphrases (the cheesier and more annoying the better) that make their way into popular culture, For example. "Give Me a Break!," Kit Kat; "I'm lovin it," McDonald's; Netflix and chill

Smell: We have a remarkable ability where our sense of smell triggers specific memories and emotions. Smell marketing is as effortless as a café wafting the scent of frying out into the street, or as complex as hotels use patented fragrances in their plane cabins, towels, and on their crew to enhance their brand experience.

Taste: Associating through your taste pallet to trigger comfort or excitement. The brand provides free samples or offers to try new food products. For example, Naturals Ice Cream, India, gives unlimited sample servings. Starbucks serves samples of any new drink they come up with.

Story: Heartstring-tugging Christmas TV ads (John Lewis, Marks and Spencer, Sainsbury's).

Factors influencing the consumer behavior toward the brand

Consumer behavior is a byproduct of myriad factors, all of which a brand may not be in control of. **Culture is a chief example of what influences**

behavior. Culture, simply put, is our attitudes and beliefs. It is developed along with age in the society. For an individual who is still growing up, his primary influences are his members of the family.

> *He learns about religion and culture via them and eventually through this, stems his opinions, attitudes, and beliefs*
> —Richard 1976

All these nuances will somehow find their way into the buying behavior of the consumer. Besides family, friends, and other acquaintances also help shape the behavior of an individual. Culture is the overriding cause of all of a person's wants and behavior. Culture is picked up from family, places of worship, school, peers, and colleagues. It is a heterogeneous mix of basic values, perceptions, wants, and behaviors. Shifts in cultures create opportunities for new products to crop up.

Social status also happens to dictate buying behavior of the consumers. Division based upon social status allows companies to position their products to appeal to people of specific social classes. Let us take the example of automobiles.

Marketing for Mercedes Benz is in sharp contrast to the marketing campaign of the likes of Honda or Toyota because they target a different set of individuals. Another powerful tool in the marketing arsenals of brands, which they often use to manipulate is the influence of social factors. To be recognized as a part of a group, or represent a certain lifestyle, one must have certain possessions. Personal and psychological factors are used in crafty manners to target very niche market segments. The broad idea is to make the product look supremely exclusive and let the same be reflected in steep prices.

What is buying behavior?
Buying behavior is the subconscious force that determines whether the consumer decides in favor of buying a product for their use or not. The few dimensions to the concept that need to be understood include:

- Why do consumers buy what they buy?
- What are the key factors influencing consumers to buy the products?
- What are the changing trends in society?

Consumer buying behavior refers to what consumers buy at a certain point in time, which involves their decision-making prowess. Hence, it is imperative for a company to keenly analyze consumer buying behaviors as it acts as the north star for a company's marketing strategy. Besides, it has a key role in the success of the company. Any firm needs to develop a marketing mix that aligns with the targeted customers.

There are few variants to the buying behaviors of customers based upon the nature of the product that needs to be purchased.

Complex buying behavior is said to occur when an individual seeks a lot of information about a high-value branded product before purchasing it.

Habitual buying behavior is where the individual buys the product as a routine habit without giving the decision much thought.

Variety-seeking buying behavior is when the individual likes to shop around and experiment with different products.

Consumer buying behavior is determined by the level of involvement in the purchase decision (Renjith June 2004). According to Mahatoo (1985), the nature of the decision process depends upon the product and the consumer.

The marketers need to determine the kind of decision-making behavior that is often involved with the particular product to decode and make sense of the behavior of the consumer. **Howard (1989) classifies consumer buying decision into three broad categories:**

1. **Routine response programmed behavior:** A routine response behavior can be seen in play when a consumer is buying a frequently purchased low-cost good or service. Such goods and services can be viewed as low-involvement products, from the prism of customer behavior because the consumer spends little to no time on decision making and purchases readily. **The quick purchase is a consequence of skipping many steps in the decision process due to a habit that almost imitates a reflex.** The consumer may be aware of the other options in the specific product category but chooses to stick to one brand.

Limited decision making: This phenomenon occurs when the customer wants to gather moderate amounts of information about an unfamiliar brand in a product category. Acquiring information about an unfamiliar product category is called limited decision making. This behavior is traceable in buying decisions involving products like books, clothes, cosmetics, and so on.

Extensive decision making: Consumers usually spend much time on extensive decision making with high involvement when they intend to purchase an unfamiliar product that demands a high capital commitment. This is the most complex type of consumer decision making as the consumer needs a great deal of information to compare it with its alternatives available. Examples of the same include cars, computers.

2. **Complex buying behavior can be broken down into three steps:**
   - The consumer develops a certain belief about the product.
   - The belief of the consumer establishes an attitude about the product.
   - The consumer makes a thoughtful choice.

   Consumers engage in complex buying behavior when they are exceedingly involved in a purchase, the involvement is caused due to the product being expensive, risky, and highly self-expressive. Many products do not carry features unless the buyer does some research. The marketer of a high-involvement product must understand the consumer's information gathering and evaluation process. And, bearing the process in mind, the marketer needs to develop strategies that will aid the buyer in learning about the product's attributes and their importance. The marketer also needs to differentiate the brand features, motivate storekeepers, and use proper media channels to describe the brand all in service of enhancing a buyer's interaction, which, in turn, influences the brand choice.

3. **Dissonance-reducing buyer behavior**: According to Herbert (1965), the consumer sometimes gets highly involved in a purchase only to find not much difference among the offerings of different brands. The high involvement is because the purchase is expensive, infrequent, and risky. For this type of purchase, the consumer will

look around to learn more about the product but will eventually base the buying decision on primary factors like price or convenience.

However, after the purchase, the consumer might experience dissonance by hearing favorable things about other brands or noticing certain disquieting features in the product chosen by him. Now, the consumer will alert the informants who support his or her decisions. For instance, here, the consumer acted first but then acquired new beliefs and ended up with a set of attitudes. Marketing communication should feed beliefs and evaluations that help the customers feel good about the brand of their choice.

4. **Variety-seeking buying behavior**: Henry (1987) stated that some buying situations are characterized by low involvement but significant brand differences. More often than not, consumers engage in brand switching. A suitable example could be that of cookies. The consumer possesses little knowledge of cookies, chooses the one that he does, and does the evaluation while the very act of consumption itself, nothing much before it. The consumer may have been able to satiate his needs, yet the next time, there exists a probability that the consumer may reach for some other brand according to his taste. Brand switching occurs for the sake of variety rather than dissatisfaction.

Steps for the Buying Decision Process

The consumers engage in the cerebral process to make sense of things in an intense marketing environment and make purchases. The consumer goes through a series of logical stages to arrive at the decision when he faces a problem that could be resolved through a purchase. A typical buying process consists of five stages (Micheal and Elnora 2000).

Step 1: Problem Recognition

The purchase process starts where the buyer recognizes a problem or need. The need may be triggered by internal or external stimuli. Marketers need to identify the circumstances that trigger a particular need (Micheal 2003). People have unsatisfied needs and wants to create tension or discomfort, which can be satisfied by acquiring and consuming goods and services.

Hence, the process of deciding what to buy begins when there is a need, and it can be satisfied through consumption. Mahatoo (1985) states that when the consumer becomes aware of a discrepancy between the existing state and the desired state, a need is aroused.

The existing state is the total situation of a consumer, the current needs, attitudes, motives. The desired state is the situation after the kinds of changes the consumer wishes. Both these states are the functions of consumer's motivation, personality, and experience of cultural and social influences.

Evans and Burman (1984) define a stimulus as a cure intended to motivate a person to act. It can be social, commercial, or non-commercial. Need recognition shows a person's readiness to act by becoming aware of a need but does not guarantee that the decision-making process will continue. Kotler (2003) suggests that by gathering information from several consumers, marketers can identify the most frequent stimuli that trigger interest in a product category, thereby developing marketing strategies that would create a spark in consumer's interest.

Step 2: Information Search

When a consumer needs to gain knowledge about a product or service, he or she would be aroused to search for more information in the product category. Consumer information sources fall under four groups:

- Personal sources: Family, friends, neighbors
- Commercial sources: Advertising, salesperson, dealers, display boards
- Public sources: Mass media, consumer rating organizations
- Experimental sources: Handling, examining, using the product

The relative amount and influences of these information sources vary with the product category and consumer characteristics (Peter, Daniel and Nancy 1986).

Customer decisions are based on a combination of past experiences and marketing information. Baker (2000) states that if there is a sufficiently high level of involvement with the problem, the consumers are likely to engage in a complex and extensive information search. If the involvement level is low, they are likely to use a very simple information search.

Kotler (2003) states that by gathering information the consumer learns about competing brands and their features. There will be a lot of brands available to the consumer in a product category, in which only a few brands the consumer would be aware of (awareness set). Among these brands, few brands will meet consumer's initial buying criteria (consideration set). As the consumer gathers more information, only a few brands would remain (choice set). All the brands in the choice set might be acceptable.

Step 3: Evaluation of Alternatives

There is no single evaluation process used by all customers or by one customer in all buying situations. Consumers view each product as a bundle of attributes with varying abilities to deliver the benefits needed to satisfy them. The attributes of interest to buyers vary by product. Once a choice set has been identified, the consumer evaluates them before making a decision. The evaluation involves establishing some criteria against which each alternative is compared. The criteria that consumers use in the evaluation result from their experience and feelings toward various brands as well as the opinions of family, friends, and so on (Stanton, Etzel and Walker 1994). The product-related attributes such as quality, durability, price, design, and so on influence the buying decision of a consumer.

A way to narrow down the products in the choice set is to pick an attribute and then exclude all products in the set that do not possess that attribute (Lamb and McDaniel 1992). Thus, the choice that possesses all the required product-related attributes can be selected.

Step 4: Purchase Decision

From the evaluation process discussed, consumers will reach their final purchase decision, which is made up of five purchase subdecisions: brand decision, vendor decision, quantity decision, timing decision, and payment method decision (Joseph and Howard 1987).

After evaluation, the first thing in mind would be to purchase the product or not. If the decision is to buy, a series of related decisions must be made regarding the features, where and when to make the actual transaction, how to take delivery, a mode of payment, and other issues. So, a decision to purchase starts an entirely new series of decisions that may be time-consuming and difficult. Selecting a source from which a purchase can be made is also a buying decision (Stanton, Etzel and Walker 1994). A consumer's decision to modify, postpone, or avoid a purchase decision is heavily influenced by risk.

The amount of risk varies with the extent of money at stake, the amount of attribute uncertainty, and the amount of self-confidence. Marketers must understand the factors that create a feeling of risk in the consumer, thereby providing information and support to reduce the risk (Kotler 2003).

Step 5: Postpurchase Behavior

Every customer after buying a product will experience either satisfaction or dissatisfaction. Hence, the marketer's job does not end when the product is bought; it must be monitored for postpurchase satisfaction and postpurchase actions. A very important stage of the consumer's decision is the impact of current decisions on future purchasing behavior.

- Satisfaction

Satisfaction occurs when a product performs according to expectations. The brand chosen has served to fulfill the customer's needs and thus reinforces the response of purchasing the brand, which also means that beliefs and attributes about the brand are positively influenced, and the likelihood of repurchase is increased.

• Dissatisfaction

Dissatisfaction occurs in the reverse situation; when the product's performance is not up to the expectation, it leads to negative beliefs and attributes about the brand. A dissatisfied customer is not likely to recommend the product to others.

The results of satisfaction and dissatisfaction are recorded in long-term memory and become inputs to the internal search of the firm. So, the marketers must be careful in satisfying the needs and expectations of the customers.

• Cognitive dissonance

Cognitive dissonance occurs when the consumer experiences a feeling of doubt or psychological discomfort about the choice made. It is often felt right after the purchase when the consumer begins to have second thoughts about the product chosen.

Dissonance is more likely to occur in complex decision making with high-involvement purchases. Dissonance can come from a personal source from an advertisement or experience with the product.

Post purchase evaluation is important to marketers because positive evaluation increases the probability of repeat purchases and brand loyalty. Negative or doubtful thoughts increase the probability that different alternatives will be considered next time when the need arises (Husted, Varble and Lowry 1989).

One can develop cognition through senses regarding the brand experiences, which can drive a decision-making/purchase-making process. What are the significant steps customers follow whenever they set out to purchase something they might read an online review, share and compare experiences with friends and family, and/or talk to employees/customers and make judgments about the brand? You cannot stop them from doing this, And why should you when you can have these factors work to your advantage? What you can do additionally is some targeted messaging and reacting swiftly to feedback. This combination of the active messaging and responsiveness that is totally in your hands, and the brand's interactions do not add to a customer's overall brand perception.

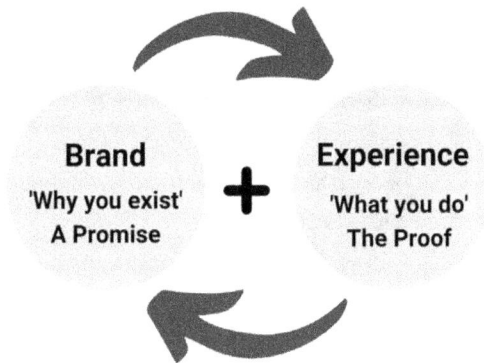

Brand
'Why you exist'
A Promise

+

Experience
'What you do'
The Proof

Because brand perception is essential to build up brand equity, a premium value a brand provides to a business—and its impact on overall revenue, sales, and profits, it's necessary to measure it consistently, track it over time, and identify what drives refinement and growth. You can do several things to measure how customers perceive your brand and, in this process, understand which areas you could improve.

One innovative way to do it could be getting groups of people together (big or small), either face to face or remotely, to hear the positives and negatives of your brand. People who use your product/services and would care enough to share their opinion (basically your band of loyal customers you have earned over the years). You 'll be able to gauge how customers feel and develop a genuine understanding of what works well and what doesn't.

A perfect example of this process happening in real time is online brand forums (particularly useful in more complex supply chains). For instance, in an B2B2C(Manufacturer to business to consumer) chain, manufacturers may find it hard to reach their end-user customers directly only with the distributors or retailers. The end-user is on the other side of the chain and hence not directly accessible. An online forum with customers fills in the knowledge gap, suggesting numerous new ways into product development and brand strengthening (through improved connection leading to various improvements in service).

Another way to get out the go about gauging customer perception is surveys. They help you understand who your customers are and what they think of your brand directly, maybe through a set questionnaire that answers all the critical questions regarding your brand. They're painless and straightforward to do; in a survey situation, customers with a point of view—good or bad—can respond to targeted questions and use open text to say what's on their mind without even having to reveal their identity. To develop substantial results and analyze the data, Net Promoter Score and CSAT can be used as reliable metrics. Ideally, a business should run brand perception surveys at least quarterly. However, it expedites the process by tying them up with advertising campaigns frequently to track how your brand efforts contribute to your brand.

People usually don't feel obliged to hold back on social media. So, what you can do is track the posts, including your brand's mention and a reaction to your branding activity across Facebook, Twitter, LinkedIn, and Instagram, to analyze your social messaging performance. When you know what people think and are saying about your brand, you can respond rapidly and grow your social presence faster. Having tools like a dashboard that monitors a brand's social presence can reveal insights such as: which social media platforms are helping your brand most; the types of content that gets popular fast; the number of mentions and the frequency of it, often in real-time; reviews, comments, and other observations; influencer reach; dwell time (how much time audience spends looking at your brand); which paid content performs best and how to optimize such payments

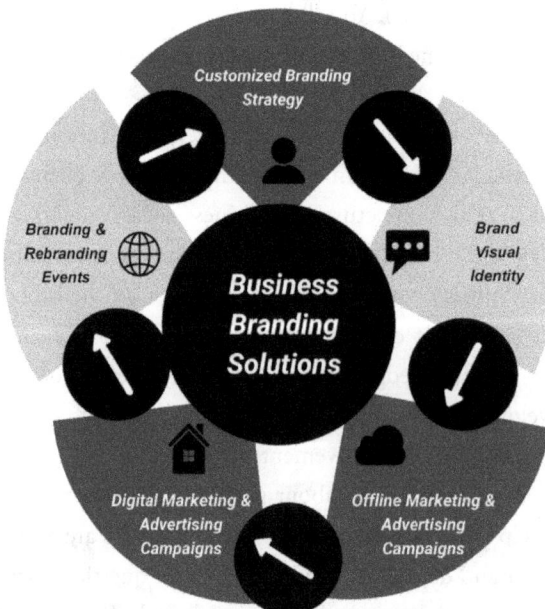

Customized Branding Strategy

Branding & Rebranding Events

Brand Visual Identity

Business Branding Solutions

Digital Marketing & Advertising Campaigns

Offline Marketing & Advertising Campaigns

Now when you know, the game is to use it properly. You have found out your brand's perception, and you know a little more than before about what resonates with those customers; you can act on your findings.

An Ogilvy study observed 20 channels and found that social media is the easiest and the quickest way to change and increase brand perception, coming a full circle from using social media to survey brand perception to using the same to improve it.

Another consumer study from Nielsen shows that for **77 percent of the consumers, family and friends' advice is the most effective and persuasive when looking for information about new products.** This word-of-mouth branding of social is part of what makes it so effective in improving brand perception.

Therefore, knowing who your customers are, what their thoughts are about your brand, and what else they are enthusiastic about give you the exact information you need to harness the power of social, word of mouth, and influencers to boost your brand perception.

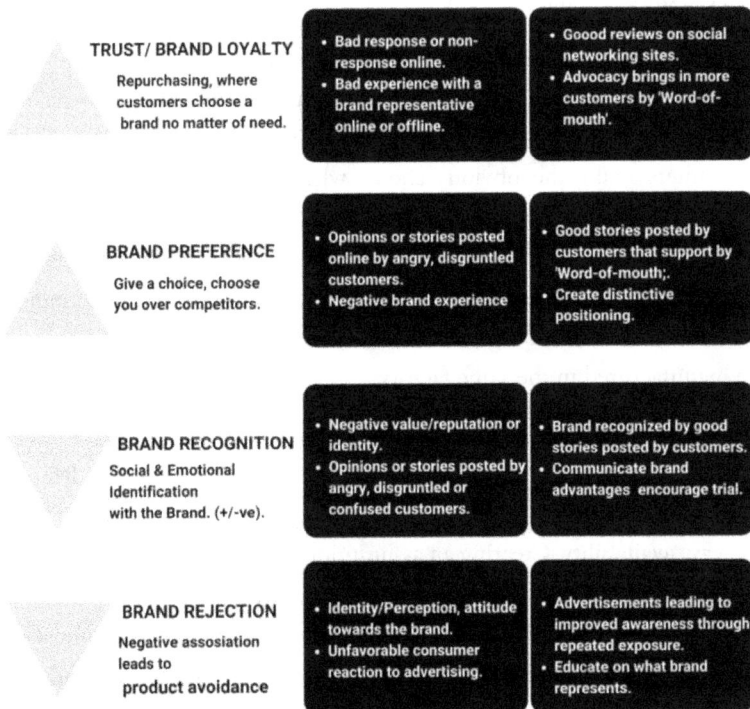

TRUST/ BRAND LOYALTY Repurchasing, where customers choose a brand no matter of need.	• Bad response or non-response online. • Bad experience with a brand representative online or offline.	• Goood reviews on social networking sites. • Advocacy brings in more customers by 'Word-of-mouth'.
BRAND PREFERENCE Give a choice, choose you over competitors.	• Opinions or stories posted online by angry, disgruntled customers. • Negative brand experience	• Good stories posted by customers that support by 'Word-of-mouth;. • Create distinctive positioning.
BRAND RECOGNITION Social & Emotional Identification with the Brand. (+/-ve).	• Negative value/reputation or identity. • Opinions or stories posted by angry, disgruntled or confused customers.	• Brand recognized by good stories posted by customers. • Communicate brand advantages encourage trial.
BRAND REJECTION Negative assosiation leads to product avoidance	• Identity/Perception, attitude towards the brand. • Unfavorable consumer reaction to advertising.	• Advertisements leading to improved awareness through repeated exposure. • Educate on what brand represents.

Here are some ways to do it:

Measure your brand's uniqueness

Every other asp brand wants to lead the way in delivering quality products and fantastic customer service; what makes your brand different? Just ask yourself and out there as to what unique you have an offer; use the accurate analytics software to analyze their words, grouping them by topic to identify the most robust associations.

You'll be able to track opinions

Track and optimize the various elements of brand perception. Brand awareness is a scale to which the target audience in the marketplace is familiar or aware of the brands in different segments. Small businesses usually find their products at a disadvantage compared with larger competitors' alternatives, backed by millions of dollars in advertising. Brand awareness has several unique effects on consumers' perceptions of different brands. So, managing to build brand awareness is crucial for small business success.

Key takeaways from this exercise is to build a strong brand perception, which results in some additional benefits

Quality

Consumers expect highly advertised brands to offer higher-quality products than generic products or brands they have not seen before. Consumers make the obvious choice when presented with a mix of options for individual products, ranging from highly advertised and recognizable brands to generic products. Shoppers are likely to view the higher-priced brands with a name as superior to generic brands (nameless), even assuming both brands contain the same ingredients or are manufactured in the same factory.

Availability

Highly advertised brands are commonly broadly distributed and more comfortable to recognize, hence a relation between well-known brands and easy availability. Creating an assumption that well-known brands can be found in a variety of outlets, let's talk about Budweiser and the Baltika. These are the brands of alcoholic beverages, for example. Consumers in the United States assume that the highly recognized Budweiser brand can be bought at any grocery or liquor store. On the other hand, Baltika can only be found in a picked few specialty liquor stores in the United States. Hence consumers in the United States looking for beer are more likely to utter that they need Budweiser rather than Baltika.

Identification

Famous brands with the highest level of brand awareness already achieved can build a sense of identity with consumer groups so that these brands are seen as marks of pride and association. For example, the Nike brand dominated the basketball shoe product category with its Air Jordans for more than 20 years. As a result, every severe basketball player felt that he had possessed a pair of Air Jordan in the product's back then to reflect his passion for the sport.

Choosing the top-notch strategy for your company to build a desirable perception is only possible when you map the parameters of your product/service and market to the appropriate model 1:1

Mind-share branding

Success in this category is achieved by owning and perpetually expressing a set of abstract associations that customers denote to the product or service. However, the perceived benefits of buying and using the products (i.e., consistently low price, great selection) are very tangible to the customers. As the company demonstrates the "brand DNA" in every transaction, it becomes firmly ingrained in the customer's mind as the only viable option in that particular product category.

Interestingly, mind-share branding works equally well at opposite ends of the product spectrum. Functional and low-involvement product categories (such as Tide, Southwest Airlines, and Wal*Mart) and complicated, high-involvement product categories (such as Dell computers) can both prosper under a mind-share brand strategy. At each end, however, the goal—and primary benefit—is to simplify the buying decision for the customer.

Cultural branding

Cultural branding is a definitive American way of all branding strategies because it uses cultural icons to establish and sustain a brand myth with which individual consumers can passionately identify. To put it succinctly in two words—"brand religion." The focus is not ever on the product or service itself and is instead on the relationship between the cultural icon and the product and the brand myth that the consumer opts for. The most successful brand myths address acute contradictions in society that echo deeply with the thought process of common people too.

Culturally branded companies can be identified in every category, ranging from home décor, fashion, and automobiles to food/beverages, entertainment/leisure, and social movements. What kind of person responds to cultural branding? It's the meek, mild-mannered accountant who buys the Harley–Davidson hog to unleash his "inner self" on weekends. It's the budding playground hoopster who just knows that he will never reach the NBA unless he wears Nike Air Jordan. It's the thirsty consumer reaching for an ice-cold Coca Cola because "it's the real thing."

Emotional branding

Want your customers to consider you a pal rather than just another random faceless entity they buy from? Then emotional branding strategy is the name of the game you ought to play. Here, the goal is to build intense interpersonal connections with each individual who interacts with the brand so that you end up with a relationship partner rather than a customer. Emotional brands have real personalities. They are often expressed through a character or persona (Mickey Mouse, Ronald McDonald) that appeals to people of all ages. Emotional brands work best with services, retailers, and specialty goods—such as Disney and Starbucks—where the company can tap into powerful emotions and create compelling experiences that evoke strong loyalty to the brand.

Emotional branding is a term used within marketing communication that refers to the practice of building brands that appeal directly to a consumer's emotional state, needs, and aspirations.

Viral branding

Courtesy of all the media buzz, viral branding has rocketed to the top of the charts as the latest brand strategy of choice. However, the fact that the media has embraced it should imply it to be an automatic choice for all the companies as well. As the name implies, viral branding works by spreading the word through "brand viruses" such as influential spokespeople, early adopters, and other forms of grassroots marketing. Accordingly, it achieves the best results with new fashions, new technologies, and premium and superpremium brands that eschew mainstream markets.

Viral branding appeals to those who aspire or resonate with the cool, hip, and with trend vibe. It appeals to those who get a charge from "discovering" a new brand and leading the bandwagon of early brand advocates. Who stands out in the viral branding category? Google, Hotmail, Absolut Vodka, and Vonage immediately come to mind.

Sensory branding

Singapore Airlines and Kellogg's Cornflakes in the same branding category? Absolutely! Hold the gaze long enough and you can fathom how exactly. Sensory branding takes the focus off the product or service itself and puts the limelight on the sensory experience it creates for the consumer. Therefore, the index entry for this category chronicles a diverse range of products and services, from fashion, cosmetics, and high-end retail to automotive and travel/hospitality.

Sensory branding goes beyond the ordinary to create a full connection with one's environment through the senses. We're talking full-on sensory engagement here! Not just with the overstimulated senses of sight and sound, but also connecting with touch, taste, and smell. In some categories, the buying experience (how, when, and where the product is purchased) helps to build the brand. Here the brand doesn't begin until customers use the product or service. The result is an experience so pristine, rich, and satisfying that customers refuse to consider any other option.

All strong brands are imbued with a clear focus on one of these models. However, while it's usually best to focus your branding efforts on one model, aspects of the other models can be cherry-picked to strengthen a brand further.

For example, the mind-share model of branding tends to rely on the sight and sound senses. But, it's wiser to add a distinctive touch or smell from the sensory model to compound further. Regardless of the strategy chosen, building a strong brand depends upon applying the appropriate model to your product category, the unique circumstances of your customers, and your market to build a perception that breeds loyal customers.

Key Takeaways

1. *Brand perception is something your consumer considers a product or service represents. It is not what the brand is saying it does. Brand perception originates from the consumers' experience, usage, functionality, dependability, and word-of-mouth recommendation—online or offline.*

2. *A brand stimulates different senses to build a particular perception— sight, sound, smell, taste, and story.*

3. *Brand perception is essential to build up brand equity—and its impact on overall revenue, sales, and profits.*

4. *It is essential to manage and measure brand perception because, according to Yotpo, 60 percent of the consumers will tell their friends and family about the brands they're loyal to.*

5. *Some brand expression tools to generate a perception are positioning, differentiation, personality, benefit and value, voice, messaging, stories, emotion, empathy, logos, typography, color, imagery, e-mails, offers, advertisements, articles, videos, and so on.*

6. *Buying behavior is the subconscious force that determines whether the consumer decides in favor of buying a product for their use or not.*

7. *Complex buying behavior is said to occur when an individual seeks a lot of information about a high-value branded product before purchasing it.*

8. *Habitual buying behavior is where the individual buys the product as a routine habit without giving the decision much thought.*

9. *Variety-seeking buying behavior is when the individual likes to shop around and experiment with different products.*

10. *A routine response behavior can be seen in play when a consumer is buying a frequently purchased low-cost good or service. Such goods and services can be viewed as low-involvement products, from the prism of customer behavior because the consumer spends little to no time on decision making and purchases readily.*

11. *Consumers engage in complex buying behavior when they are exceedingly involved in a purchase, the involvement is caused due to the product being expensive, risky, and highly self-expressive.*

12. *The consumers engage in the cerebral process to make sense of things in an intense marketing environment and make purchases. The consumer goes through a series of logical stages to arrive at the decision when he*

faces a problem that could be resolved through a purchase—problem recognition, information search, evaluation of alternatives, purchase decision, postpurchase behavior.

13. *A most efficient way to measure brand perception is to survey with your stakeholders, employees, customers, and an open market survey. This approach allows insight into current and potential buyers.*

14. *Another way to measure brand perception is to sign up for Google Alerts to monitor the Web for any mentions.*

15. *According to Nielsen, more than 84 percent of the buyers say that they moderately or entirely trust peer recommendations. So, it is a good idea to monitor online reviews to get valuable insights about your brand.*

16. *Measure your brand presence on social media and engage with your consumers. According to socialmediatoday.com, 33 percent of the consumers prefer to reach out to a business via social media to express their experience about the brand.*

17. *De Chernatony (1998) has listed four tools for measuring the brand image.*

18. *Projective techniques are helpful if customers are unable or unwilling to express their opinions. These methods include image interpretation, brand personality descriptors, and sentence completion. For, example, displaying a picture of a man driving his new BMW into a golf club's parking lot to interviewees and asking, "What do the other people in the picture think and would say about the man driving a BMW?"*

19. *Another projective technique is brand personality descriptors, which are used to describe a particular brand's consumer, for example, by completing the sentence: "The typical driver of a Ford Fiesta is......." (De Chernatony 1998; p.406). Sentence completion consumers should be used to complete the following kinds of sentences: "I buy a personal computer, I look for...," for instance.*

20. *Qualitative techniques (De Chernatony, 1998; p. 406) free associations can be used to find new associations and further research during group discussions or in-depth interviews.*

21. *Through evaluations and beliefs ratings, it is possible to try to find out consumers' views on critical attributes and the strength of their associations with specific brands.*

22. *Comparison of brand associations is applied for confirming the identity of the comparative weaknesses and strengths of the brand. An example of this is asking the interviewees to identify different juice brands, ask them to define which one they believe to be the best or worst one, and explain why it is better than the other brands (De Chernatony 1998).*

23. *Mind-share branding works equally well at opposite ends of the product spectrum. Functional and low-involvement product categories (such as Tide, Southwest Airlines, and Wal*Mart) and complicated, high-involvement product categories (such as Dell computers) can both prosper under a mind-share brand strategy.*

24. *Culturally branded companies can be identified in every category, ranging from home décor, fashion, and automobiles to food/beverages, entertainment/leisure, and social movements.*

25. *Viral branding appeals to those who aspire or resonate with the cool, hip, and with trend vibe. It appeals to those who get a charge from "discovering" a new brand and leading the bandwagon of early brand advocates.*

26. *Emotional branding is a term used within marketing communication that refers to the practice of building brands that appeal directly to a consumer's emotional state, needs, and aspirations.*

27. *Sensory branding goes beyond the ordinary to create a full connection with one's environment through the senses.*

CHAPTER 9

Overview

The study on the significance of branding on a company level has been verified in the previous chapters. However, this chapter strives to bring light on personal branding, which is a more novel concept few are acquainted with the power of. Personal branding stands for the process of creating an individual brand identity to build a better consumer reputation in a way similar to that of a large product, and service brand would use to build its brand. Some examples of successful personal branding are discussed, segregating them into two categories of first-movers and industry leaders. Going on to discuss the personal traits for people successful in personal branding and how they did it along with some thought-provoking statistics on the reputation of personal and global brands in the eyes of consumers. An interesting discussion on how empowering employees to build their brand can offer measurable benefits to the individuals and the organization does open up the doors to various lucrative opportunities. After understanding the concept of how personal branding gives one an edge over competitors, added benefits like constant growth, profit, confidence, leadership, and credibility are discussed. The impact of creating professional associations with strong personal brands is measured, which improves your personality and image and stands out in an otherwise saturated market of competitors and influencers. The chapter closes with some tips on how to create and grow one's brand successfully to offer the world a value that is limited to an individual's oneself.

Personal Brand

Personal branding is about managing your name—even if you don't own a business—in a world of misinformation, disinformation, and semi-permanent Google records. Are you going on a date? The chances are that your "blind" date has Googled your name. Were you going to a job interview?

—Ditto.-Tim Ferriss

Personal branding stands for the process of creating an individual brand identity to build a better consumer reputation in a way similar to that of a large product, and service brand would use to build its brand. Personal branding is a one-man band. This recognition is a relatively recent movement and has been fueled by the advent of the Internet, allowing individuals to amplify their fame and use this very fame to drive business and career outcomes. Personal branding can be seen as an essential and vital strategy for professionals across all industries.

A BRAND

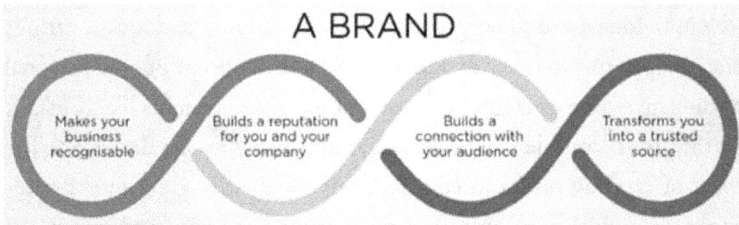

Makes your business recognisable | Builds a reputation for you and your company | Builds a connection with your audience | Transforms you into a trusted source

The idea sounds like a great way to go. Now let's focus on the ways to do such branding. However, there are multifarious ways to get about the task. A brand should forge a multipronged strategy to go about the same.

Some examples of successful personal branding:

In this time of the Internet, it's becoming increasingly easy to become famous without any real claim to fame, cough, the Kardashians, cough. So, if you think of the most renowned business people today, they can generally be categorized into one of two segments:

1. **First-movers:** They are the first-mover or a leader who became recognized for their innovation, ingenuity, or business success. Let's

have a look at some real-life examples—Mark Zuckerberg, Steve Jobs, Jeff Bezos, Elon Musk, Bill Gates. But, you don't need to be the first person to put millions of songs in someone's pocket to achieve business success.

2. **Industry leaders:** These are the people who have driven huge business success through their personal brand's smart use. Instead of creating a name for the business, they made a name for themselves. They then leveraged that for their business. Examples here would include Gary V, Tim Ferriss, Neil Patel, and so on.

Personal traits for people successful in personal branding

- Consistent content creation and curation
- A lifelong entrepreneurial inclination
- Authorship built the foundation of a unique brand
- Drive for constant growth and improvement
- Risk appetite
- Luck and opportunity
- Ability to recognize new opportunities

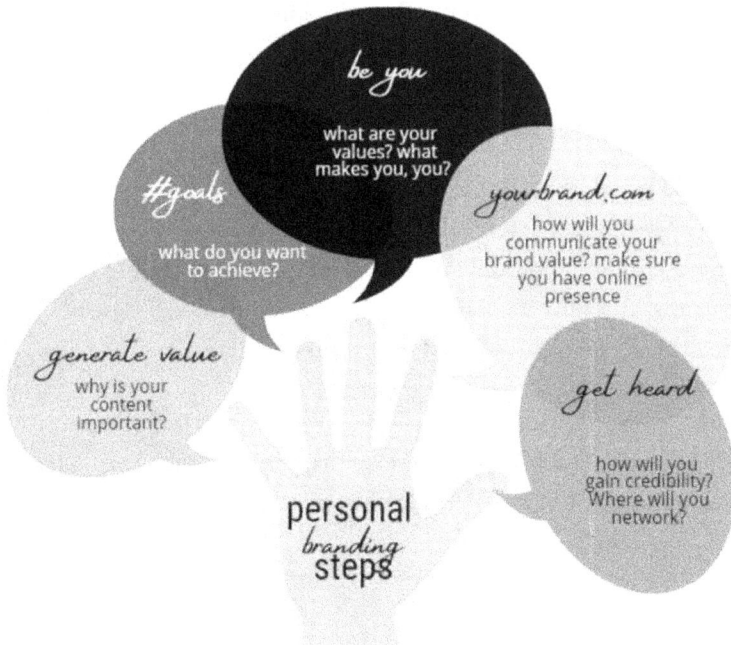

Additionally, businesses that help employees build a strong personal brand are the largest gainers from this concept. Such tendencies help your brand positively. The same holds even for entrepreneurs. A business founder's personal brand makes his or her startup noticeable. Business success is also about credibility and trust. Consumers want to feel positively toward the leadership or the core team of a business. Here are thought-provoking statistics in 2019: 56 percent of the worldwide consumers say they now trust local brands more than global brands, a 13 percent increase since 2015. This higher number is possible because a local business has a face and a personality associated with it.

Small businesses and even large organizations encouraging personal branding have strengthened corporate branding both internally and externally. And, when employees (any employee from CEO to essential staff) successfully brand themselves as experts in the industry, both employees and the company they serve can achieve measurable benefits, to name a few: increased visibility, industry knowledge transfer, trend identification, stronger collaboration, leadership development, improved brand perception.

We have understood by now that personal branding gives you an edge over your competitors and makes an everlasting impact on the individual. But, that is not all why personal branding is essential.

There are more reasons to it.
Growth
Personal branding brings growth because it makes you and your product noticeable in the market. Personal branding does open up the doors to various lucrative opportunities. When you possess a brand of your own generates a positive response and contributes to overall development, drawing people toward you, wanting them to get associated with you.

Profit
When the personal brand nourishment happens, it results in enrichment at the corporate and individual levels; you actualize 100 percent of your

most precious asset—your human capital in this scenario. By empowering yourself or your employees to build their personal brand and nurture the corporate brand in the process, everyone can impact revenue and generate equity.

Confidence

For the possibility to bag an opportunity and amplify the chances of leveraging it to your best, some confidence must be built and flaunted. Being a brand of your own gives the required confidence, which further makes it possible to grab the opportunities and make the most out of them.

Credibility

The credibility that gets attached to a personal brand infuses and goes a long way. Some celebrities are brands, and they do promote products/services. They hold that position because of the credibility that branding has bought. Understand this with an example: you are scrolling through your Facebook feed, and you see a wall of sponsored content with company names. You're probably not going to click any of them, but if you see a piece of content, blog, or an article that your friends shared or a celebrity shared, authored by a real human being, the click-through rate is going to be higher. We are social animals simply desiring to hear from each other.

Leadership

In successfully building a personal brand, one indeed becomes a leader in the area he or she specialized in. The takeaway is that you shall remain to be ahead of others because others follow you. Given the advantage of your personal brand achievements, you shall be in a leading position already.

Highlights

Working on personal branding helps you first realize, then highlight your achievements, objectives, skills, and interests. Engaging the target audience at a greater level and telling them precisely what you can do for them.

YOU OWN YOUR
ATTITUDE
The attitude that you
decide to have towards
your business is the
attitude that truly defines
your personal image.

ENTHUSIASM
SELLS
Very few methodologies
sell better than offering
excellent professional
services that transmit
enthusiasm.

SELF IMAGE
The image that you hold as
a carwash business owner
or operator is the reflection
of what you believe you are
and you are the image of
what you hope to become.

TRUST AND SUCCESS
NETWORKS
Our reputation may begin
with us, but it is anchored in
our contacts and the
connections we have with
others.

SUCCESS DRAWS
FROM SUCCESS
Remember, carwash
customers like your
business because it makes
them feel good. Focus on
providing honest and
genuine business strategies.

IMPORTANCE OF
CONTACTS
Building a network of trust
requires establishing
long-term relationships
with people who appreci-
ate us and whom we
appreciate in return.

HALO OF SUCCESS
In the end, carwash
customers and employees
will belive what you say
about yourself so it's
important to avoid
negative statements and
always be positive.

BUILDING
NETWORKS OF
TRUST
Organize your list of
contacts, update your
current contacts and renew
ties as needed to build your
own network of trust.

POSITIVE
COMPLICITY
Treat everyone the same
regardless of job position
and responsibilities.

THINK LONG-TERM
If you wait to build your
network of trust until you are
ready to start a new
business or until your
current business is in dire
need of help, you are setting
yourself up for failure.

10

05 · 06 · 04 · 07 · 03 · 08 · 02 · 09 · 01 · 10

**ESSENTIAL
PERSONAL
MARKETING
METHODS**

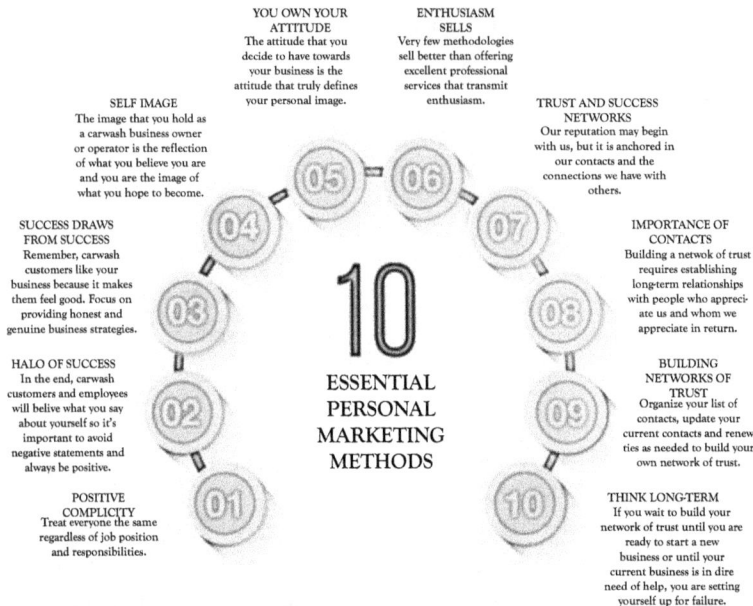

Larry Linne rightly said in his book "Brand Damage – It's Personal," it's important to lead, train, and encourage personal brand management. It won't happen on its own. And, it won't be done well without you as a guiding force.

We know from our previous chapters that a brand is a feeling and a subjective one. Talking about **McDonald's**, everyone has a particular outlook on this brand based on their unique knowledge, experience, and socio-cultural reality. Talking of McDonalds reminds us of children; even children dream of being famous one day. Until now (before the Internet boom), this was equal to winning the lottery, but the Internet has created an opportunity for more unconventional paths to fame and fortune.

Today, every other person out there is a micro-influencer, and it's now becoming more accessible to find ways to catapult oneself to stardom with a personal brand. Fortunately, the opportunity is much more com-prehensive than this, and personal brands can be practical tools whether you're trying to become the next celebrity or merely trying to sell.

The Internet has given us an outreach, allowing individuals to use social platforms to forge personal relationships with people as far as the opposite end of the globe. These connections have driven fame and fortune to the unlikely and allowed many to transcend the conceived limits to form a universally relatable brand, recognized and most importantly loved.

Here are the key steps that roughly go into such construction: identifying strengths and passions; identifying the desired outcome; becoming a subject-matter expert; selecting key social platforms; frequently sharing content and delivering value, resultantly build a community, and the final stroke is connecting your personal brand to business outcomes.

How to Define Your Personal Brand

What type of content will you be posting? Written, visual, etc.

What are your values and how do you want to get them across?

Who is your current audience and what kind of audience would you like to attract?

What do you want to achieve with your brand?

What are you most knowledgeable and passionate about?

What tone of voice would you like to use?

How will you best communicate your message to your target audience?

Who are you, and what is your position in the industry?

Here are some tips for developing your personal brand. The preceding steps give a fair amount of ideas regarding what to do. There is something that specifically has to be done well in the previous steps.

Building an online presence of yours is gradual and vital. Use various social media platforms to develop your company and make it known. It is advisable to study the venue well before and then decide. You have an array of social media platforms; choose wisely. Communicating well is another vital aspect. You are making your thoughts known, and opinions heard. Working on communication skills and body language helps a great deal in getting the message through to your audience. Introspection is something that we shouldn't neglect. Forget about other people and things for a while, and focus on yourself. Study your strengths, weaknesses thoroughly, and work to remediate flaws. Mold them positively and present it as a complete brand. Make yourself available and accessible through possibly a website of your own. Do it well. Make sure it highlights your skills and strengths. Make use of some networking skills and create associations with stronger counterparts of yours.

Creating professional associations with strong personal brands improves your personality and image.

In a highly competitive world, it is significant to create your own space and identity. Following the mentioned steps shall help you create a personal brand of yours that shall contribute to your future development.

Embark upon the journey of being a personal brand and figure out what value you can offer the world that no one else can.

Key Takeaways

1. *In a world run with Google being everyone's best friend, rest assured that everyone expects you to be visible when they search you online.*

2. *Personal branding is just as crucial as any organization's branding and helps you first realize, then highlight your achievements, objectives, skills, and interests.*

3. *The Internet has created vast opportunities with unconventional paths for everyone to try their hands on to fame and fortune.*

4. *In a highly competitive world, it is significant to create your own space and identity.*

5. *The Internet has made almost everyone an influencer, with greater accessibility through social media platforms, to forge personal and professional relationships with people globally.*

6. *Personal brands can prove to be practical tools whether you're trying to make a difference through your initiatives to support better lives, become the next celebrity, or merely trying to sell your products/services by establishing your business online.*

7. *It is a very strategic manner of displaying yourself, your worth, and the value you can add to the world on a personal and exceptionally professional note.*

8. *Selecting the correct platforms and curating apt content is just as important as studying your strengths and weaknesses to highlight your skills and expertise.*

9. *A relatively new phenomenon, but it is essential to attract the best career and business outcomes.*

10. *Common traits that have been established by people who have forged successful branding include consistency, entrepreneurial mindsets, authenticity, constant growth, improvement, risk appetite, and the ability to recognize and seek new opportunities.*

11. *The two categories of these successful individuals are: (a) first movers, recognized for their innovation, ingenuity, or business success, and (b) industry leaders who invested in personal branding and utilized it to grow their businesses successfully.*

12. *Large companies and startups can profit from encouraging the personal branding of their employees.*

13. *Both employees and the company they serve can achieve measurable benefits such as increased visibility, industry knowledge transfer, trend identification, strong collaboration, leadership development, and improved brand perception.*

14. *There has been a large jump in preference from global to local brands, all based on the trust generated by people's personality associated with the products/services being sold.*

15. *Personal branding brings growth, making you and your product visible in the market and enhances the chance of lucrative opportunities.*

16. *Empowering yourself or your employees to build their personal brand helps make an accumulated positive impact on overall profits.*

17. *Owning your brand brings vast opportunities and provides one with a boost of personal confidence, highlighting their level of expertise in return allows them to establish trust in you to indulge in their projects effortlessly.*

18. *The credibility that gets attached to a personal brand infuses and goes a long way, as it leaves a more profound influence on your known circle than what celebrities or even experts may endorse.*

19. *Leadership is a hidden blessing and responsibility that comes with your personal brand, so be sure to uphold that reputation.*

20. *One must initiate personal branding strategically, and if possible, with guidance as once your image is already displayed out there, it won't change or get removed from the big Internet.*

21. *A personal brand is power and privilege, which evokes others' feelings like any market brand. The best part is, you have the choice to write that story because it's about you ultimately!*

22. *Just the way McDonald's happy meals evoke the emotions of joy as high as "winning the lottery," your personal brand must produce an attraction that encourages others to want to associate with you.*

CHAPTER 10

Overview

The preceding chapters have explicitly discussed the essence of branding and its importance, along with cases of successful and unsuccessful examples. This chapter aims to define artificial intelligence (AI), simplifying its true meaning, along with inspecting its attributes that equip it to be an effective tool to facilitate efficient branding to create successful businesses. AI powers tools to perform the tasks that humans typically perform. Companies can use AI to analyze data to determine customer behavior and patterns. It allows easy access to consumer behavior based on a history of their previous purchases with extremely feasible methods of cost reduction through automated workflows, intelligent analysis of data, and streamlined customer service operations.

Optimizing machine learning helps create better experiences along with narrowing down and refining the sales funnel. A closer look is extended on how Accenture helped Manzoni to drive more value from its advertising, by providing intelligence data science and machine learning algorithms, allowing them to double its forecast accuracy, saving costs, and increasing its ability to qualify users. AI has made it easier to collect and analyze customers' data based on their previous purchases, thereby making it easier to derive consumer patterns and behavior, making it convenient to discern the target audience for a particular product. A further discussion on how customer happiness and satisfaction are critical to any brand's success because happy customers ensure a firm and stable position for the brand, making it capable of standing firm despite competition disruptions that come up day after day. This connection can be achieved by harnessing the potential of AI. It is a promising technology, which holds opportunities and possibilities that can make a world of difference.

Artificial Intelligence

What Is AI?

AI is

the simulation of human intelligence in machines that are programmed to think like humans and mimic their actions. The term may also be applied to any machine that exhibits traits associated with a human mind such as learning and problem solving

—Investopedia

The term was first coined by John McCarthy in 1956; it is an umbrella term that holds various aspects of technology like machine learning, language simulation, neuron nets, and so on.

According to the English Oxford Learning Dictionary, AI is *"the theory and development of computer systems able to perform tasks normally requiring human intelligence, such as visual perception, speech recognition, decision-making, and translation between languages:*

AI is a promising technology, which holds opportunities and possibilities that can make a world of difference. The impact of this potentially revolutionary technology is felt across the different fields, the traces and echoes of it throwing innovative waves to a relatively bright future.

"Can Machines Think?" This simple question put forth by Alan Turing is what opened the doors of thought to AI. Turing's paper, "Computer Machinery and Intelligence" laid the foundations and established the vision and goal of AI as a field of study.

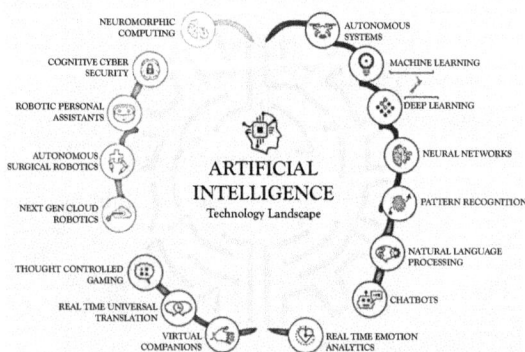

ARTIFICIAL INTELLIGENCE
Technology Landscape

NEUROMORPHIC COMPUTING · COGNITIVE CYBER SECURITY · ROBOTIC PERSONAL ASSISTANTS · AUTONOMOUS SURGICAL ROBOTICS · NEXT GEN CLOUD ROBOTICS · THOUGHT CONTROLLED GAMING · REAL TIME UNIVERSAL TRANSLATION · VIRTUAL COMPANIONS · AUTONOMOUS SYSTEMS · MACHINE LEARNING · DEEP LEARNING · NEURAL NETWORKS · PATTERN RECOGNITION · NATURAL LANGUAGE PROCESSING · CHATBOTS · REAL TIME EMOTION ANALYTICS

What makes humans different, or rather what gives them dominance over machines, is their ability to think and act rationally and default humanly. And, AI is about building a bridge where machines' technical efficiency and specialization can shake hands with the human aspects of rationality and thinking, thereby opening a pathway for development and progress that is of immense potential and promise.

AI-powered tools are used widely by businesses to accelerate their growth rate and profits while ensuring a better standing in the fields concerned. Because as the age-old saying goes, "Change is the only constant," and harnessing the core of this change is the key to consistency, as ironic as it sounds.

"Can Machines Think" has made humans think for a very long time, with diverse answers and debates, and today, we have reached a certain level of clarity with regard to that answer. A solution with a lot of underlying questions.

Importance of AI Adoption

Business is a field that is most affected by change and competition every single day. And, it is of utmost importance that they are prudent enough to anticipate these changes, update and upgrade themselves so that they can stand firm and erect while the wave of change hits. And, it will also add to their advantage if they can leverage the developing technologies blending them with their business strategies to polish their efficiency and achieve better results. This is where AI enters the scene.

AI powers tools to perform the tasks that humans typically perform. The only difference is that two new characters are added to this story, namely speed, accuracy, and a potential error-free performance; all the ingredients required to brew the best seller. A 2017 PwC report indicates that it is agreed by almost 72 percent of the business decision makers that AI will create a competitive advantage. In other words, it can act as an absolute game-changer with a speed boost to the finish line.

AI has abilities that can prove to be beneficial to the business, enhancing its profits and growth. AI can process large sets of information, thereby translating data, enabling a deeper level of human analysis. It can also automate customer interactions and improve their overall experience,

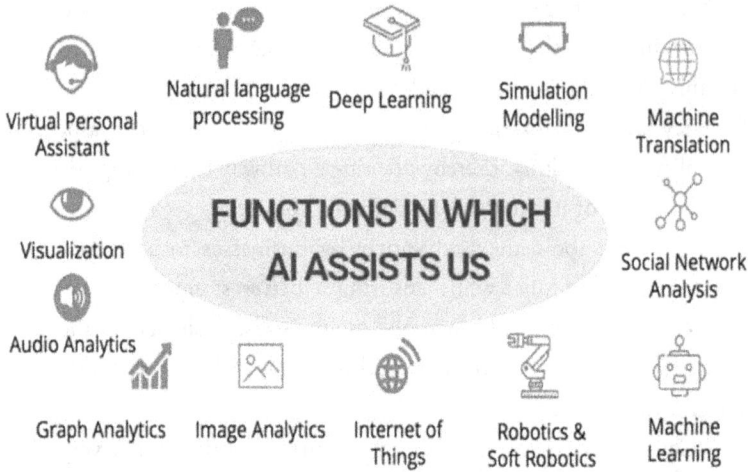

Virtual Personal Assistant · Natural language processing · Deep Learning · Simulation Modelling · Machine Translation · Visualization · FUNCTIONS IN WHICH AI ASSISTS US · Social Network Analysis · Audio Analytics · Graph Analytics · Image Analytics · Internet of Things · Robotics & Soft Robotics · Machine Learning

thereby ensuring customer satisfaction and loyalty. It also provides personalized and customized services to the target customers while also identifying potential customers who will prove to be an asset to the business.

And, these points of merit will prove to be most useful if the businesses adopt them at the earliest because when it comes to technologies of specific future potential. It is always the phrase, "Early bird catches the worm," implying two other essential aspects of a business: risk-taking and prudence. AI, machine learning, and so on might seem like uncertain waters at present; however, a business's success lies in its ability to shoulder this risk.

The following are different ways in which AI proves beneficial to the business, underscoring the significance of adopting AI.

Targeted Marketing Strategies

Consumer behavior changes over time because with changing times and better living conditions, demands take newer dimensions. The businesses must weave strategies to fit and fill these growing demands.

Companies should structure marketing campaigns to find a direct path to reach the ideal market. AI makes this path easier using various tools like data collection software, chatbots, advertising plots, and so on.

WHAT MAKES A PERFECT CHATBOT?

THE BRAND MESSAGE IS CLEAR

DOES NOT DIRECT AND REDIRECT

ASKS SIMPLE AND CONCISE QUESTIONS

CLEAR CTA

SPOT ON RESOLUTIONS

VALUE ORIENTED

AI helps analyze social media and search history to determine customer trends to direct the marketing in that path, which will be the most profitable, ensuring immense returns, one of the business's critical goals here to stay. Some of the famous names known for harnessing these benefits of AI are Netflix and Amazon.

The critical element that sets AI apart from the rest is that it adds a personal touch to the marketing strategies, where customized services and personalization act as lighthouses that lead the ship's course.

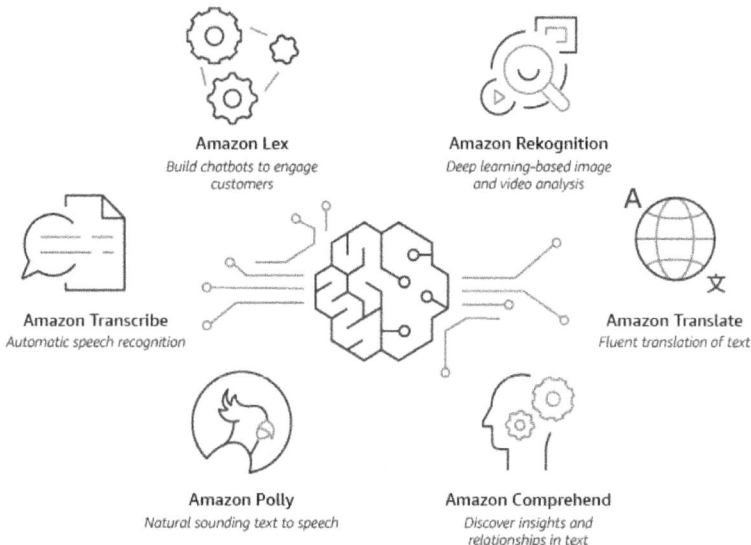

Amazon Lex
Build chatbots to engage customers

Amazon Rekognition
Deep learning-based image and video analysis

Amazon Transcribe
Automatic speech recognition

Amazon Translate
Fluent translation of text

Amazon Polly
Natural sounding text to speech

Amazon Comprehend
Discover insights and relationships in text

Refining and Narrowing Down the Sales Funnel

Companies can use AI to analyze data to determine customer behavior and patterns, which helps identify the sales leads that are most profitable and more likely to generate greater returns, thereby ensuring efficient deployment of essential resources and minimizing wastage of the same to a bare minimum. And, the higher the amount of the data, the greater the program's chances to perfect itself, highlighting why AI is called "intelligent."

Cost Reduction

AI achieves cost reduction through automated workflows, intelligent analysis of data, and streamlined customer service operations.

1. Automated workflows

Time is a significant factor, not just for a business but also for everything concerning life. **The right timing can go a long way in determining the results of various actions. However, time is a resource that we cannot control but can coordinate and use effectively.** Automated workflow enabled by AI helps cut down the repetitive and continuous tasks demanded of the human workforce, thereby providing them with more time to devote to other activities and services. It always reduces the errors and faults that are default characteristics of any human action.

2. Data analysis

Intelligent decisions are the foundations of any successful business, and smart choices call for sharpness and precision with minimal flaws and errors. AI helps manage and organize a large amount of data, making it easier for humans to analyze. Data analysis helps develop better pricing strategies, the potential areas where the operational costs can be reduced, and to uncover and rectify inefficiencies in production.

As mentioned, all these points underscore the importance of adopting AI in businesses to empower and effect change, making a world of difference characterized by efficiency and intelligence.

Use of AI in Advertising

Advertising is a crucial element for any business that is of equal importance to both manufacturers and consumers. The more innovative and mind capturing the advertisement, the better its chances to spread its branches and experience firm and robust growth. In short, promotions, when done right, give a substantial speed boost for the product or the business, which rocket it to the heights of success. And, good advertising does not happen overnight. It involves a lot of brainstorming, efforts, and creativity, blending to tailor the right strategy.

Given the significance of advertising for a business, it is only imperative that advertising is characterized by adapting itself and redesign according to the changing demands. And, blending AI advertising is a brilliant way to achieve this end because the novel and efficient abilities of AI enhance the sharpness and skill of advertising.

At present, AI is taking the world of advertising by storm, redefining and restructuring its boundaries, opening new horizons, widening its scope and reach, and adding more unique dimensions of potential. This progress is mainly achieved by AI-powered tools to analyze large amounts of data available, thereby discerning and determining customer patterns and behavior, thereby arriving at the right strategies with the help of thorough knowledge about where to tap to attain the maximum return.

This increases the efficiency of advertising to a great extent, saving costs and resources while ensuring maximum and immediate return, which is the ultimate goal of any advertising action.

Different Ways in Which AI Is Used in Advertising

Advertising Platforms

Social media is a word of routine today; its traces are evident in most humans' lives. And, it is only wise to channel this as a pathway for attaining advertising goals because it ensures maximum reach and scope. Digital marketing has, over the years, proved itself to be a profit inducer, merit it holds because of the technical efficiency, speed, and accuracy that can augment human intelligence.

Advertising on platforms like Instagram, Facebook, Snapchat, and so on uses AI in the background, supporting it to scale new heights.

Creating the right ads with skill and innovation is only part of the game because the picture becomes complete only when it is balanced with the right timing and display. How many times an ad is displayed and at what times might sound like a simple action with meager significance; however, it might come as a revelation that these two are the key elements of advertising.

And, when talking about timing, it is essential to understand that using the "out of sight, out of mind" mantra and repetitively hitting the audience with the same ads would not help. Instead, it will prove to be harmful to the campaign. This is where AI displays its prowess for sharp and measured moves. AI-powered tools discern the right frequency for an ad to be communicated to the audience through analyzing and decoding the user feedback, thereby achieving the expected impact on the audience. This goes a very long way in determining the budget effectiveness and performance of a business.

Performance and Cost

Performance is a term with multiple implications. It is not just about putting the best foot forward. It is also about absorbing the best from around, moving in sync with the change, and utilizing the space for improvement, thereby polishing the actions to attain the maximum possible perfection. And, AI chimes in its brilliance here with its ability to optimize performance. It uses algorithms to observe and analyze how the different ads perform across other platforms, their impact and influence, and by default, providing practical ways to improve and enhance performance. It even identifies specific fields or places with a potential for improvement and growth.

Some of these platforms also wisely use AI to automate actions, thereby saving time and costs. This time-saving attribute of AI-powered media enables the human workforce to focus better on other significant work, eliminating the need for manual guesswork and speculation, replacing it with precision and certainty, which paves the way for better efficiency.

Audience Targeting and Ad Creation

It is the age where hard work is replaced by smart work, ensuring better returns and success. And, when it comes to advertising, it is essential to identify the target audience and work in sync with their preferences, interests, and demands, which keeps evolving. To understand these three aspects, it is essential to delve deeper into the customer history, past purchase patterns, the changes, however, minute they are, and then curate suitable marketing strategies. However, it will be a Herculean task to do this manually, excluding the fact that it will be time-consuming and monotonous, draining the managers. Therefore, it is only imperative that AI is the perfect fit for the job, with its ability to analyze large amounts of data.

AI-powered systems also can curate ads depending on the audience and the target of the business. This is already in use on various social media platforms that use automation to suggest ads.

And, now, the inevitable why and how part of the story. Conveniently enough, there is a single word that can answer both these questions. The same term is of peak importance to businesses across the globe. Like the pragmatic theory in the literature that took the literary world by storm, this particular term has become the spotlight of importance over the last few years; **personalization**.

It is a simple term with far-reaching implications. Customer-oriented perspectives add a bigger chance for businesses to establish a firm position in the market because ultimately, it is the customers who become the advocates of a brand. Therefore, it is of utmost importance to brands to ensure customer loyalty. Moreover, this is done by providing customized services matching their preference so that they feel at home with a particular brand, thereby leaving a mark that will bring them back over and over again.

And, AI is the perfect tool to achieve this end.

How?

AI connects you with the right audience.

AI enhances customer experience and satisfaction.

AI Connects You With the Right Audience

AI has made it easier to collect and analyze customers' data based on their previous purchases, thereby making it easier to derive consumer patterns and behavior, making it convenient to discern the target audience for a particular product. This connection is of utmost importance because it adds precision to the marketing perspective, rendering it effective and efficient with minimum loss of essential resources, thereby saving costs while attaining an even more significant investment for the business in the form of the right customers.

AI Enhances Customer Experience and Satisfaction

Customer happiness and satisfaction are critical to any brand's success because happy customers ensure a firm and stable position for the brand, making it capable of standing firm despite competition disruptions that come up day after day.

And, to ensure customer satisfaction, it is essential to develop and nurture an emotional connection with the customers. You can achieve this connection by harnessing the potential of AI. The data collected about the purchases makes it easier to provide tailor-made services for particular customers, fulfilling their choices and preferences, making them feel special and unique, thereby ensuring a memorable and noteworthy position for the brand in the market.

Anticipated Benefits from using AI in Marketing

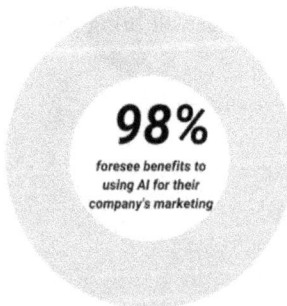

98%

foresee benefits to
using AI for their
company's marketing

**Top Benefits to Using
AI for Marketing**

Providing better insight on
accounts

Providing more detailed
analysis of campaigns

Identifying prospective
customers

AI's role in content marketing

"Tomorrow Sleep" Boosted its Web Traffic by 10,000 Percent

Tomorrow Sleep is a sleep system startup. It started generating and building content quickly after its launch. They hoped to attract a large number of visitors to their website via content marketing.

Even after publishing unique, high-quality, and useful content for many months and manually tracking and analyzing different keywords, the number of users on their website were on average, around 4,000 per month.

Some may say it was a decent achievement; it was not going to work out for them. As they had to compete with long-standing players in the already full sleep market, they had to up their numbers to make some difference.

Tomorrow Sleep had to find a suction to plan and produce customized and targeted content at a large scale.

Solution: Artificial intelligence!

Tomorrow Sleep started to use this AI-powered content intelligence and strategy platform—MarketMuse.

MarketMuse is AI-generated support for generating content strategies. So, Tomorrow Sleep utilized this AI research application to identify and understand the high-value topics they should publish. It also provided them with information on their competitors and their ranking for each of the suggested topics.

This information highlighted the gaps and opportunities in their current plan, resulting in Tomorrow Sleep building content about the identified vital topics, establishing itself as an expert.

The outcome:

- There was an increase in Web visits by 10,000 percent, that is 400,000 visits per month.
- With a single search result, they were ranked for multiple positions.
- Domain authority also obtained Google's featured snippet for exceptional results.

This AI tool found out the exact topics Tomorrow Sleep required to attract their target audience. Also, giving clarity on the competition positioning on those topics. It provides AI-generated SEO recommendations with insights that help companies to develop useful content.

2. Discovering the Value of Data in Advertising

Manzoni discovered an 80 percent improvement in its inventory forecasting accuracy with the help of AI

Manzoni is an advertising sales agency, which aimed to become a data-driven company. They started adopting new digital models for both their businesses—traditional and digital ads.

To better monetize the digital content from the pay-business model and ad-funded model, they wanted to leverage AI. They had to identify the unique targeted audience within the general segment—by age, gender, interest, and so on to succeed in this endeavor to reach out to them with particular and value-driven marketing and advertising campaigns of their brand.

Digital advertising revenue is to surpass the trading models very soon. And, this market is predominantly run by a few handfuls of Over The Top giants. They leverage targeted, highly personalized advertisement campaigns for their customers. And, this change had brought up the need to adopt AI to compete with the digital giants and rejuvenate traditional models' revenue.

Manzoni partners up with Accenture for its experience transforming businesses through AI to reach their goal quicker in an efficient manner.

Solution: Machine learning!

Accenture brought together its experience in the media industry, data monetization, and AI to meet Manzoni's goal.

Accenture armed Manzoni with data from internal and affiliate digital property to create high-valued micro-segments, resulting in targeted advertising Business to business model (B2B) and Business to Customer (B2C) digital marketing models. Manzoni adopted a high-performance machine learning platform tailored to their specific needs with specific advertisement industry cases. Catered by the Data Monetization Engine, it is one of the Accenture Multimedia Advertising Platform (AMAP).

Being a cloud-based infrastructure, it minimized the operational expenditure by a lot.

The outcome:

- There was an 80 percent increase in its inventory forecasting accuracy than before.
- As certified by ComScore and Nielsen—Manzoni's prediction of gender is at 80 percent precision.
- Based on (Internet Advertising Bureau) IAB standards, Manzoni identified 180 commercial segments that can cater to.
- Generated higher monetization because of their ability to narrow down their target audience.

Manzoni is the example of a leader willing to embrace the latest in ad tech to enhance user experiences and extend the reach and effectiveness of ads.
—Michele Marrone, Communications, Media and Technology
Lead for Italy, Central Europe, and Greece

By providing intelligence data science and machine-learning algorithms, Accenture helped Manzoni to drive more value from its advertising. Manzoni doubled its forecast accuracy, saving costs, and increased its ability to qualify users. They were resulting in a better market share and premium pricing.

3. Managing Google Ads via AI
AI generated twice the engagement with half the cost
InstantTeams spent a big chunk of their budget on their Google AdWords campaigns. But, it struggled to get returns from it. Allocating additional capital on live experimentation was not an option. Their B2B sector was very aggressive, and they required quality inbound engagement from companies seeking to build a remote team.
Solution: AI audience model!
InstantTeams built an AI model, where it used their previous campaign data, ideal for examining advertisements before going live.

By listing search ads of competitors, the brand could obtain insights that AI predicted remained more likely to be noticeable and of higher engagement for their audience. They also revealed notions for their new advertisement text by using AI to analyze their competitor ads. These AI recommendations proposed more focus on employer-friendly terms in their advertisements text.

The outcome:

- InstantTeams gained double advertisement engagement through less than 50 percent of cost compared to previous campaigns.
- Targeted Google Search Ads dramatically outperformed market benchmarks, with 65 percent more engagement at 66 percent less cost.

Let us have a look at one more:

350 percent lift in impressions via design-focused advertisement
FortyFiveSearch created high demand with a 350 percent lift in impressions and 30 percent click-through rate for InteriorDefine.com with junction AI predictions and insights.

InteriorDefine gives its customers the capability to design their sectionals online and get straight away home delivery. After running a non-branded Google AdWords campaign, including extremely competitive keywords for sectionals, they looked toward AI to improve their ad results and better their traffic and engagement results.

Solution: AI audience model!

- After testing their ads on AI audience model, they discovered that their ad score improved drastically by eliminating the second headline.
- By implementing AI insights "Start," "Design," and "Online," FortyFiveSearch formed a different Headline 2 with a call-to-action "Start Designing Online" for InteriorDefine. Those, as mentioned, changed the performance prediction score from a − 1 to a +3.

The outcome:

- InteriorDefine's click-through rate rose by 30 percent, with a 350 percent increase in impressions. Employing junction AI, the company saved time and energy in optimizing the advertisement to generate demand.

You can see how the companies leverage AI to generate demand and engage better with their audience. But, let us talk more about brands creating their value via bettering **user experience.**

Some of the big names that are heard in connection with AI like Google and Microsoft only validate this technology's undeniable potential that can rocket the market position with astonishing power. Amazon, IBM, Facebook, Apple, and so on come under the long list of names where AI research has become the primary objective. Their position attests to the fact that they are on the right path among the customers and the market.

Some AI tools that help in brand implementation:

1. Rosebud
Rosebud's AI technology generates customized **"human models"** for your brand advertising campaigns. Because of this AI-generated marketing tool, companies are not dependent on talent. Based on your target audience, market, brand tone, you can build a "model" that connects better with your audience. This provides a cheaper and quick option to create more effective advertisements. Rosebud's technology maintains that their AI-generated models prove a 22 percent increase in the click-through rate.

2. Synthesia

- Synthesia is a localized and personalized video-generation tool using AI. They offer two solutions:
- Translate the video content to over 99 languages, including the video's person, to appear talking naturally in either of these languages.

They are personalizing communications with customers. With Synthesia's AI technology, an AI person in the video interacts with the customers individually—like by mentioning their name and any other precise information.

3. Pencil
Pencil is an AI text-generation tool for headlines and descriptions.

Using the information you provide about the brand, audience, product, and so on, it automatically generates headline options and product descriptions in the correct tone of voice, with the brand essentially being unique to each audience.

4. Phrasee
Phrasee generates marketing text for social media, push, and e-mail campaigns, to get a better open rate, conversions, and clicks. AI generates messaging that is true to the brand's voice, as a result, resonating well with the audience. Virgin Holidays claims that with the use of Phrasee's AI, their e-mail revenue has increased by a few million pounds. Domino's Pizza also recognizes that their e-mail results have enhanced impressively after leveraging the Phrasee solution.

AI enables companies to create highly personalized customer experiences cost-effectively compared to other high-investment branding campaigns.

Machine Learning Algorithm Used by Google

Google adds to its brand value by using AI to provide more accurate results for each user, providing a better user experience. Delivering the best outcome for each user is deeply rooted in its brand prism, so it makes sense to leverage AI to take it up a notch.

Similar to Siri from Apple, Google uses AI to power its assistant on smartphones. AI helps generate better suggestions and recognize patterns unique to its users, which Google uses to provide information on events, e-mails, or any information they will be more interested to see.

Personal Fitness Advisor by Under Armor

Under Armor uses IBM Watson to build a health tracker application "—"Record." It tracks and analyzes your workouts, routine, sleep data, and nutrition intake. It also imports data from other fitness tracking apps. As a result, it provides personalized recommendations for training and nutrition for its users. By this use of AI, Under Armor has changed the way people can explore fitness advice by essentially providing personal trainer knowledge without going to the gym.

The Music You Love on Spotify

Spotify uses AI and deep learning, like every music or video streaming app. It uses AI to give recommendations on related music that users will appreciate. AI observes the music listening choices and includes them into the learning algorithm to generate better song suggestions. Spotify shows suggested songs based on the sort of music a user listens to more regularly. This use of AI may not be as advanced as other companies. Still, it uses predictive analytics and AI algorithms to learn about each user, enhancing the product and brand experience.

Some more example of AI in action:

1. **Netflix**: Uses AI to provide personalized recommendations based on their user's viewing habits. It uses AI to review each of its videos to compress it only to the degree necessary without compromising the quality. More than 80 percent of TV shows watched were discovered through the platform's recommendation system.
2. **Sephora:** It has a chatbot giving out beauty advice on Kik messenger. Based on the information gathered regarding consumer's product preferences. It shares advice and product suggestions as a soft sales model.
3. **Starbucks:** It allows users to place and pay for orders using Alexa. My Starbucks Barista is a voice assistant built to take, modify orders, and confirm the pick-up location.
4. **Facebook:** Its Deeptext understands text with near-human accuracy. Facebook uses AI to stop fake news to go viral. It uses a deep neural network for ad placements. In 2017, Facebook rolled out an AI project that can identify people with suicidal tendencies. It has a high accuracy rate of 97 percent for facial verification.
5. **Apple:** Apple uses deep learning to detect an attack on the Apple store and face detection in iOS10. It uses neural science to face

recognition to unlock the phones and transfer the expressions to the emojis.

6. **BMW:** BMW connected is an opt-in system and personal mobility companion that gathers data about customers and their car. BMW creates a mechanism that can see like humans in collaboration with Intel. Along with its partner, Here Maps, BMW is helping automated cars learn everything about the locations.

Key Takeaways

1. *AI is "the theory and development of computer systems able to perform tasks usually requiring human intelligence, such as visual perception, speech recognition, decision-making, and translation between languages."*

2. *AI powers tools to perform the tasks that humans typically perform. The only difference is that three new characters are added to this story, namely speed, accuracy, and a potential error-free performance; all the ingredients required to brew the bestseller.*

3. *AI helps analyze social media and search history to determine customer trends to direct the marketing in that path, which will be the most profitable, ensuring immense returns, one of the business's critical goals here to stay.*

4. *Companies can use AI to analyze data to determine customer behavior and patterns, which helps identify the sales leads that are most profitable and more likely to generate greater returns.*

5. *AI achieves cost reduction through automated workflows, intelligent analysis of data, and streamlined customer service operations.*

6. *Advertising is a crucial element for any business that is of equal importance to both manufacturers and consumers. The more innovative and mind capturing the advertisement, the better its chances to spread its branches and experience firm and robust growth.*

7. *Advertising on platforms like Instagram, Facebook, Snapchat, and so on uses AI in the background, supporting it to scale new heights.*

8. *AI-powered tools discern the right frequency for an ad to be communicated to the audience through analyzing and decoding the user feedback, thereby achieving the expected impact on the audience.*

9. *Companies use AI algorithms to observe and analyze how the different ads perform across other platforms, their impact and influence, and by default, provide practical ways to improve and enhance performance. It even identifies specific fields or places with a potential for improvement and growth.*

10. *The time-saving attribute of AI-powered media enables the human workforce to focus better on other significant work, eliminating manual guesswork and speculation.*

11. *AI tool found out the exact topics Tomorrow Sleep required to attract their target audience. Also, giving clarity on the competition positioning*

on those topics. It provides AI-generated SEO recommendations with insights that help companies develop useful content, resulting in an increase of 10,000 percent in the Web traffic.

12. By providing intelligence data science and machine-learning algorithms, Accenture helped Manzoni to drive more value from its advertising. Manzoni doubled its forecast accuracy, saving costs, and increased its ability to qualify users. They were resulting in a better market share and premium pricing.

13. With AI's use, InstantTeams gained double advertisement engagement through less than 50 percent of the cost compared to previous campaigns.

14. InteriorDefine's click-through rate rose by 30 percent, with a 350 percent increase in impressions. Employing junction AI, the company saved time and energy in optimizing the advertisement to generate demand.

15. A chatbot is estimated to save over eight billion USD annually by 2022.

16. It is projected that AI-powered autonomous vehicles can help save 300K lives on the road within a decade.

17. According to IDC, a market research firm, global spending on AI systems is said to reach 57.6 billion USD in 2021.

18. AI has made it easier to collect and analyze customers' data based on their previous purchases, thereby making it easier to derive consumer patterns and behavior, making it convenient to discern the target audience for a particular product.

19. Customer happiness and satisfaction are critical to any brand's success because happy customers ensure a firm and stable position for the brand, making it capable of standing firm despite competition disruptions that come up day after day. You can achieve this connection by harnessing the potential of AI.

CHAPTER 11

Overview

Almost everything that we use in today's world, from our smartphones with Google Navigation, to washing machines, to the most convenient and fun addition to daily lives—Alexa, they are all wonders of artificial intelligence (AI), which has transformed the potentially disastrous innovation into additions to the daily lives of humans. This chapter revolves around several aspects of artificial behavior and explains theories connected to it in humans' personal lives, consumer behavior, businesses, and business environments. It begins with deep-diving into various models of consumer behavior such as the economic model, learning model, psychoanalytic model, sociological model, and the Nicosia model. Then, further progresses into exploring the impact on awareness with AI. For businesses, making use of the right tools becomes key to enhancing brand awareness and upholding high value for your consumers to succeed continuously. AI helps provide personalized experiences and fast solutions to consumers, keeping their loyalty and satisfaction high. Moving onto the potential of optimizing marketing engagements with the application of AI enhances the whole process and experience with the use of deep learning, targeted advertising, chatbots, speech recognition, and of course, curated recommendations. This creates a specific emotional bond between the customer and the brand, at the same time ensuring technical efficiency and cost benefits. AI can work from the grassroots level to the top, with the potential to change the game altogether, whether it be customer satisfaction or genius marketing strategies.

Artificial Behavior

Humans' one line of distinction from the rest is a mind's presence, with its logical, analytical, and emotional attributes. It's the very reason why a man is called a social animal. And, that is why for a long time, this was the trump card for humans over any machine for machines might fill the analytical and, to an extent, logical criteria; however, the realm of emotions is still under the dominance of a broadly thinking and speaking community that comes under the species of Homo sapiens.

However, the world is evolving, and just like the Hegelian concept of individual and universal souls, being a part of the whole means being a part of that evolution as well. Man's first encounter with technology that had broader horizons beyond that of the natural world, which could curate a new world was with the advent of the wheel, the traces of which are still evident today. And today, on the dawn of a more contemporary world with better perspectives and newer technologies with the potential to change humanity's face.

And, among them, what shone the brightest with certainty to defeat the long haul of uncertainties is artificial intelligence or popularly known as AI. Two simple alphabets, the simple solution to a multitude of questions, and an equation that can balance everything from science and technology to business and marketing.

Since we have narrowed down our focus on branding and effective brand-building strategies and how to effect a change in the organization and profits, it's time to sharpen our line of vision with better insight into how AI manages to strike down the right targets necessary for a brand to establish a firm position in the market.

Before we dive into AI behavior, let us understand consumer behavior first.

Schiffinan and Kanuk (2004) defines consumer behavior as "the behaviour that customers display in searching for, purchasing, using, evaluating and disposing of products and services that they expect will satisfy their needs."

The Economic Model

According to the economic model, the customer may be a rational man, and his buying decisions are completely governed by the concept of utility. The model assumes that the buyer is conscious of the multiple alternatives available in the market; he has the knowledge and skill to rank all different offerings, and he finally takes a rational decision. He makes a choice after taking under consideration the value and benefit. For example:

Price effect: Lesser the price of the product = more quantity purchased.
Income effect: Higher income or surplus money = more quantity purchased.
Substitution effect: Lesser the price of the substitute product = lesser the utility of the original product bought.

The Learning Model

According to the learning model, consumer's buying behavior is highly affected by manipulating the drivers, stimuli, and responses of the buyers. The model is based on a person's ability of learning, forgetting, and discriminating.

Unlike the economists, psychologists argued that humans are influenced by both innate needs like hunger, thirst, sex, shelter, and learned needs like fear and guilt. The various products or services (brands) acts as stimuli to satisfy these needs. When consumers learn to associate the connection between stimulus and response, it becomes a habit.

The Psychoanalytic Model

The psychoanalytic model is based on Sigmund Freud's theory of personality that human behavior is the result of the interactions among three component parts of the mind: the ID (instant gratification), ego (rational), and superego (moral compass). According to this model, a consumer has a multiplex set of deep motives that drive him toward specific buying decisions. The buyer has some hidden fears, desires, and wishes. His buying action can be affected by appealing to these desires.

The Sociological Model

According to the sociological model, the individual buyer is influenced by society, by inmate groups, as well as social classes. His buying decisions aren't completely governed by utility, he features a desire to emulate, follow, and fit in together with his surrounding environment. Several consumers' buying decisions could also be governed by societal compulsions.

The Nicosia Model

The Nicosia model created for marketers belongs to the category called the systems model where the consumer is analyzed as the system, with stimuli as the input to the system and behavior as the output of the system. It tries to establish the link between a firm and its customers, how the activities of the firm influences the consumer and results in the buying decision.

Each model is unique and explains the consumer behavior and its triggers. AI helps brands understand the wants and preferences of the consumer through this behavior analysis. It predicts the purchasing behavior of their target audience.

As we have seen in the earlier chapters, the extra unique gem for AI makes it crucial, and that it caters to consumer behavior. In turn, this helps provide personalized services, thereby ensuring customer satisfaction and loyalty, which are crucial to the survival of a brand in the long run.

Effective use of data by analyzing customer preferences and purchase patterns helps to discern the right target audience, which helps achieve efficiency and prudence, attested to any successful organization's significant characteristics. The personalized services create a sense of belonging in the customers beyond the mechanical or technical consumer–producer relationship and cross over to the realm of human emotions. It draws in the necessary elements to grow and channel them in the right way, thereby blending the right amount of logic, reason, and emotion into building a work field with fertile soils where fruits of success and development are guaranteed.

This emotional element, however, poses a contradiction as well. A paradox can seem complicated but can nevertheless be broken down into simple pieces of perception through the available technology's right and efficient use. While emotional AI successfully moves forward, exploring novel fields to work on and attain higher levels of development and success, humans' position is questioned. When machines take over the emotional ground, which was earlier the realm of humans alone, what will be the implications? Will they be beneficial in the long run, or would they be paradoxically dangerous? This leads to a probable obsoleteness of human skill sets that predominantly draw their power from this very human relations element to human relations, which runs more profound than the frozen waters of machinery and technology. Because with the evolution of technology, the frozen waters are being warmed up for better and more efficient use.

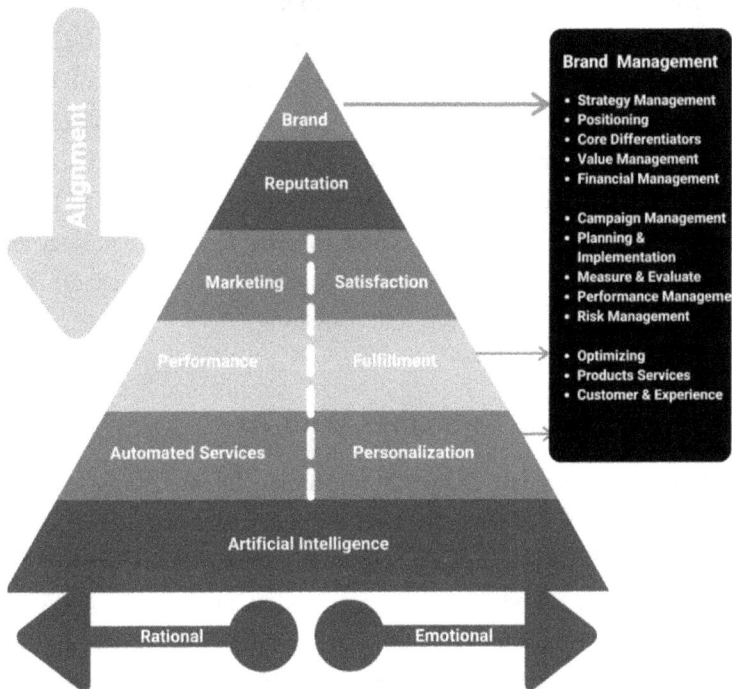

This complication, or rather, the dilemma, might make one reminisce about Darwin's theory of survival of the fittest.

However, the answer lies in the preceding statement itself. The human-to-human connection will stand despite the advent of machine learning since a company's persona, which again comprises a part of what the brand is, is highly dependent on its employees and even more on the company culture. Because a company's growth and stature are not just about the sales and marketing strategies, it runs deeper than that.

The company culture builds the company's face, which is highly dependent on the human workforce, thereby making the recruitment process even more crucial. And, it is at this point that the human and machine work in harmony. The proper use of AI can help select the right candidates, which might not always be possible with a traditional recruitment process. And, in this way, by ensuring the sharpness of selection, AI again builds a strategy for creating an amiable company culture, which helps attract customers' right kind and sustain the same.

According to futurist and author Blake Morgan, AI will be part of almost 95 percent of the customer interactions by 2025. This attests to the fact that AI helps in connecting to the customers at an emotional level. By tapping into data that is already provided through previous interactions with the company, AI helps draw a clearer picture of its needs and wants, thereby allowing the brand to upgrade and personalize its services. This creates a specific emotional bond between the customer and the brand that will remain strong throughout since it enhances the sense of loyalty in the customer while at the same time ensuring technical efficiency and cost benefits. This way, AI creates the right emotion, which can help tremendously in brand building and marketing.

Awareness With AI

With every passing day, competition assumes different forms, and the efforts to stay on top of the grid are no less than a fierce battle. Every company judiciously plans out and strategizes the next move so that every step taken is firm and fair while at the same time leaving a mark of its own.

Therefore, we must use the right tools. And, when it comes to the right tool, brand awareness is always the first word in the dictionary for success. In straightforward terms, brand awareness "is the extent to which customers are familiar with the offering, qualities or image of a particular brand of goods or services." Branding is no less than an art, and it's essential to use the right colors so that the canvas is unique and special and something to which the consumer is attracted repeatedly. Because, for a company, its brand is its mouthpiece, the one thing that speaks for it, and the umbrella under which all its functions are brought together. And, briefly put, a brand is a unique signature that distinguishes it from other products and services of a similar nature. And, the line of distinction is the unique blend of the company's personality added to the brand. The uniqueness that's invariably recognized by the target customer if it is utilized in the right way.

The more the customer is familiar with the brand, the more the chances are for the product's better standing in the market and, more importantly, its survival in the market. When brand awareness is done with finesse and precision, it acts like a magnet that attracts potential customers to the company and retains them while simultaneously serving as a shield against the increasing competition and products in the market.

However, for a brand to be crowned with adjectives like "trending" and "popular," it is essential to plan with prudence while being in sync with the time and technologies and consider the consumer, whose choices ultimately decide the future of the brand. So, inevitably the next question is, how?

Choices initially present a picture of flexibility and better opportunities. However, the more the number of options, the greater the need for accurate deployment of those very choices because the right choice can rocket your product to the top, while the wrong one can affect a disastrous avalanche.

Marketing is what creates a ground for the product, a firm foundation where it can grow and prosper while at the same time, it also acts as a crutch during times of distress and loss, which helps the product to keep standing despite the circumstances. If marketing is the ground, then advertising is what gives wings to the business. Every potential customer must be made aware of the product, and above all, the product must secure a position of primus inter pares. And, the key to that is the utilization of the right tools.

In this age and day, when every sunrise promises a more significant advancement in technology, we must be wise enough to exploit it in the right way. Because the old school rules are being upgraded, and we must elevate ourselves as well. One example of such a groundbreaking technology is AI. AI is not a precarious set of questions anymore. The years of critical experimenting and learning has transformed AI from a questionable field of science to an area that holds answers to a lot of difficult questions. As defined by John McCarthy, AI is "the science and engineering of making intelligent machines." Humans are deemed superior species because of their ability to think and analyze past experiences and develop insights that could be applied in a future scenario by inferring the past. A human experience strikes a chord with anyone, whether it be a customer or anyone who seeks anything. And, AI does precisely this. Add to the capacity to infer from patterns the dexterity and efficiency of a machine. That squares the crucial role AI can play in brand building and brand awareness. AI can work from the grassroots level to the top, with the potential to change the game altogether, whether it be customer satisfaction or genius marketing strategies.

Even the best marketing techniques won't bear fruit without customer satisfaction. A customer is most satisfied when he or she is made to feel special and it evokes certain emotions.

And, this is where AI comes in by providing a personalized experience and fast solutions to their queries. This is done through voice and speech recognition, the ability to predict consumer behavior and emotions. This also allows the companies to be in a position to provide personalized recommendations as well, thereby creating the first successful step in brand awareness. Because loyal and satisfied customers can speak for the brand, thereby enhancing its standing in the market.

AI can also significantly contribute to effective customer care because retaining customers is as important as gaining them.

Marketing engagements can go a long way in taking your brand to the next level. And, with the application of AI, this potential is enhanced. One example of this is targeted advertising, which helps provide personalized recommendations to the customer at an earlier stage of the purchase. Every customer appreciates a brand that is insightful about their needs.

All said and done, AI can add a stroke of success to your brand if utilized in the right way. Every business is a blend of critical and creative thinking, with a tint of human perception and understanding. And, we must think about the times. And, since a business is a prime runner in the race of success, one cannot stress the significance of keeping up the pace any further. Technological innovations can smoothen the roads to win, but that happens when we are ready to embrace these roads.

Thus, every entrepreneur needs to understand that change is the only constant. And, the consistency of their business is directly proportional to how they move along with the changes.

According to the Harvard Business Review, "A.I. systems and devices will soon recognize, interpret, process, and simulate human emotions. A combination of facial analysis, voice pattern analysis, and deep learning can already decode human emotions for market research and political polling purposes."

This provides a more apparent foresight into AI's potential that can transform the face of marketing itself. Two simple words, with one massive possibility of change and transformation, and it's up to us to embrace this change because everything successful was once a streak of innovation upheld by people with a belief in evolution.

Let's move forward from this chapter with a reflection on the words spoken by Annette Zimmerman, Vice President of research at Gartner, in January 2018, "By 2022, your device will know more about your emotional state than your own family."

Key Takeaways

1. *With heavily saturated and highly competitive markets, it is only natural that everyone is pushing their limits to stay on top.*

2. *Accepting and adapting to technology trends is essential as creatively maintaining the human touch through these growing innovations.*

3. *Every growing individual, entrepreneur, and business must embrace constant change and the dynamic nature of human minds and markets to maintain directly proportional efforts to keep their value intact.*

4. *Making use of the right tools becomes key to enhancing brand awareness and upholding high value for your consumers to succeed continuously.*

5. *Branding is an art, and making use of an impactful aesthetic increases brand recall and keeps consumers hooked to come back repeatedly.*

6. *A brand is a unique signature that distinguishes its personality and the quality of a unique experience that stands out from other products and services of a similar nature.*

7. *Remember that the better acquainted a customer is with your brand, the better value and longevity your products and services will have in the market. It will also protect your brand from increasing competition and potential external risks associated that could hamper your business's growth or image.*

8. *Schiffinan and Kanuk (2004) defines consumer behavior as "the behaviour that customers display in searching for, purchasing, using, evaluating and disposing of products and services that they expect will satisfy their needs."*

9. *The economic model assumes that the buyer is conscious of the multiple alternatives available in the market; he has the knowledge and skill to rank all different offerings, and he finally makes a rational decision. He makes a choice after taking under consideration the value and benefit*

10. *According to the learning model, consumer's buying behavior is highly affected by manipulating the drivers, stimuli, and responses of the buyers. The model is based on a person's ability of learning, forgetting, and discriminating.*

11. *The psychoanalytic model is based on Sigmund Freud's theory of personality that human behavior is the result of the interactions among*

three component parts of the mind: the ID (instant gratification), ego (rational), and superego (moral compass).

12. *According to the sociological model, the individual buyer is influenced by society, by inmate groups, as well as social classes. His buying decisions aren't completely governed by utility, he features a desire to emulate, follow, and fit in together with his surrounding environment.*

13. *The Nicosia model created for marketers belongs to the category called the systems model where the consumer is analyzed as the system, with stimuli as the input to the system and behavior as the output of the system.*

14. *Effective use of data by analyzing customer preferences and purchase patterns helps to discern the right target audience, which helps achieve efficiency and prudence, attested to any successful organization's significant characteristics.*

15. *A large number of choices for both businesses and consumers can seem like great opportunities. However, it can be confusing to deploy or select profitably. Hence, keeping a keen eye on making the right choices can ensure no rash decisions are made that could be a cause of regret.*

16. *We can see one of the greatest innovations made by humans to date in the form of AI.*

17. *If utilized wisely and efficiently, AI has the power to obtain high levels of success for your business. It helps you stay in the game of "latest trends" and "coolest" products.*

18. *Everything that we use in today's world, from our smartphones with Google Navigation, to washing machines, to the most fun addition to daily lives—Alexa, they are all wonders of AI, which has transformed the potentially disastrous innovation into significant parts of our daily lives we cannot imagine surviving without.*

19. *John McCarthy aptly describes the term as "the science and engineering of making intelligent machines."*

20. *Despite a great wave of automated services that have hit the new generations, as humans, we still seek the warmth and experiences that make us feel connected.*

21. *AI plays a massive part in the choices individuals make today, which is created with personalized experiences by collecting unbiased data from a vast audience.*

22. *That is something humans cannot do, as we are complex beings with our own opinions.*

23. *AI can work from the grassroots level to the top, be it customer satisfaction or genius marketing strategies for building brand awareness.*

24. *AI helps provide personalized experiences and fast solutions to consumers, keeping their loyalty and satisfaction high.*

25. *Optimizing marketing engagements with the application of AI enhances the whole process and experience with the use of deep learning, targeted advertising, chatbots, speech recognition, and of course, curated recommendations.*

26. *AI also gives excellent insights on potential improvements and helps analyze overall business performance.*

CHAPTER 12

Overview

Post the introduction to the workings and a host of benefits that come with artificial intelligence (AI), it is crucial to keep a note of the drawbacks as well. This chapter predominantly aims to exhibit the limitations and reliability of AI from a present and futuristic perspective. The human world and minds are flawed, whereby there are great attempts to create the illusion of perfection, however still leaving room for reflection and reinvention. Important factors like the lack of human element limited to no creativity, limited access, feasibility, high risk, inability to self-sustain or evolve, and potentially harming human value by choosing machines must be considered. The clear distinctions between human and machine capabilities are explored. The only thing that separates humans from the rest is their intuitive and conscientious abilities, which can help them makeshift when necessary, which is an impossible attribute for machines. Boiling down to the fact that machines are capable of doing intense physical and calculative, repetitive work that multiple humans together may find confusing and exhaustive. After a certain point in time, it can even affect the quality of the work, as humans are wired with physical, mental, and emotional needs. On the other hand, machines cannot work creatively, as it requires an active and present conscious mind, which is absent in AI. AI technology is also very expensive and hence is not a feasible option for the masses, and if it goes wrong, holds high risk in terms of money and potential failure that could have large-scale adverse effects. Choosing to create betterment for the world and humans by degrading the value of a human is questionable.

AI Limitations

According to the famous Carl Gustav Jung, "Wisdom accepts that all things have two sides."

Ever since AI has manifested itself in technology, it's abundant potential has also thrown questions. Whether the vast world of AI is a threat or a blessing has been a matter of debate since forever. And it's essential to understand both sides of the story before tapping into its resources. Even the ocean bed that holds the world's most precious pearls is filled with dangers that can prove life-threatening if not cautious and aware.

And, it's only a given that to make effective use of AI, it's essential to be well versed with the different sides, the good and the bad.

The human world is not one of absolute perfection; flaws are inherent, no matter the tremendous and never-ending efforts to create an illusion of perfection. Because flaws are human, and it is these very flaws that leave space for reflection and reinvention. And, artificial intelligence, though bestowed with qualities and characteristics that can surpass human abilities, means that humans create it with flaws. Since it goes through that human filter, it will have traces of those flaws that are human and those that are innate due to its distance from what is "human." Contradictions again are a part of the world we live in. It's best to understand these in their depth, thereby reaching a better level of knowledge that can be used to understand the world and its workings better.

The benefits of AI are numerous, and this is evenly balanced out by the disadvantages, which are briefly discussed as follows:

The cost barrier: AI is a sophisticated technology that is still evolving with a potential for both success and failure. And, this a risk that is innate in any innovative step. There is no moving forward, the chance of a step forward or a fall, and without this risk. Due to the complicated machinery involved, the installation costs alone are huge, and this is followed by the repair and maintenance costs, which aren't exactly affordable to all. While at the same time, to attain maximum efficiency and sharpness, constant upgrading of the software must be required according to the changes and evolving fields of action. And, the story doesn't end there. The costs become even more in case of a potential breakdown, this probability of which cannot be avoided. All said and done, AI is a deep dive into the mysterious ocean. And, unless one is ready to face the highs and lows, it wouldn't be wise to take the jump.

The lack of the human element: No matter what, the creation can never imitate the creator. Humans make errors, they have short-comings, but all these imply another crucial element that draws the line of distinction between humans and the rest. It is the presence of conscience or the ability to distinguish between what is right and what is wrong. From this very conscience and consciousness, humans' ethical and moral sense stem from, both of which are crucial to survival in a social environment. And, this is what the machines lack. Despite every-thing, AI is still "artificial." Therefore, they aren't rational or moral and cannot be relied upon for decisions and choices around the legal and ethical framework.

The failure to upgrade and evolve: Humans make mistakes, but these mistakes also give them a space for improvement and innovation, which is why it is rightly said that "Failures are the stepping stones to success," and AI lacks these very stepping stones. They can efficiently perform one function repeatedly; however, changing and upgrading themselves according to the constantly changing environment is beyond their scope and capability, which again points to their inherent lack of human element. There is no human touch or sense of belonging or passion, the moral and mental attributes that contribute to the success and growth in the long run.

The question of creativity: Creativity is what adds a unique hue to the human palette of skills. It is said that with the right amount of creativity, even science can become poetry. It is a rare gem bestowed upon humans to make order out of chaos, to find a streak of beauty with just a gaze of passion. And, this is what machines lack. They do not work based on creativity since creativity requires an active and thinking mind, which will be absent in AI. Machines work efficiently but not creatively. They follow the commands and instructions but thinking outside the box will always be the forte of humans.

The threat of unemployment: The inherent threat of human skills being obsolete when taken over by machines is another massive question on the face of AI and its advances. And, the problem is relevant even today. Is it okay to turn a blind eye to humans for the betterment of humanity? Then, what about the critical fact that it is the parts that comprise the whole?

These chain reactions of questions will continue as long as progress is a part of our society. The ultimate question is whether we are prepared to take that leap of faith. We must traverse unknown waters and strange roads to reach the beautiful destination.

We must also turn our focus to an important truth unveiled by all those disadvantages of AI stated earlier. Each one of those implies the importance of finding a balance between machines and humans, which is the only way through which either of them can cancel out the flaws of the other and work toward maximum perfection because harmony is what keeps us going, whether it be between humans and humans, humans and the environment, or for that matter, humans and machines.

And, let us not forget what Elbert Hubbard said, "One machine can do the work of fifty ordinary men. No machine can do the work of one extraordinary man."

Key Takeaways

1. *The human worlds and minds are flawed, which try to create the illusion of perfection, but continuously leave space for reflection and reinvention.*
2. *It is essential to understand that anything that could be a boon could also prove to be a bane if not utilized cautiously.*
3. *The way technology has manifested its way into our lives with phases of controversies about its benefits and failures, AI has also trodden the same path. Though it has a list of services that can never be undermined, it is vital to beware of its shortcomings.*
4. ***The cost barrier:*** *AI is an innovation of a kind but calls for complicated machinery that comes with high installation costs, followed by repair and maintenance costs for both physical and software-related upgrades to ensure smooth functioning. There is also a potentially high risk associated with it, not just in the form of money but also the risk of failure, which has no turning around.*
5. ***The lack of the human element:*** *The first term "artificial" immediately gives away a big loophole. It is rightly said that the creation can never imitate the creator, and since humans have their own shortcomings, it automatically leaves scope for flaws in any man-made design.*
6. *The only thing that separates humans from the rest is their intuitive and conscientious abilities, which can help them makeshift when necessary, an impossible attribute for machines. They are incapable of making choices that have not already been fed to their systems through planned algorithms.*
7. ***The failure to upgrade and evolve:*** *Machines can efficiently perform one function repeatedly; however, changing and upgrading themselves according to the constantly changing environment is beyond their scope and capability. There is no human touch or sense of belonging, passion, compassion, and neither ethical foundations nor emotional characteristics that can support individuals or organizations with their success and longevity.*
8. ***The question of creativity:*** *Machines do not work based on creativity, as it requires an active and present conscious mind, which is absolutely absent in AI. The ability to work fast, cost, and time efficiently is a plus. However, machines don't have a mind of their own and are incapable of*

any creative-oriented input/output. It is somewhat a master and helper dynamic, where machines follow the commands and instructions but cannot contribute anything outside their predetermined capacities.

9. ***The threat of unemployment:*** *Humans have contributed to civilizations and growth by toiling and laboring for thousands of years. Before the first machines were introduced, humans manually did everything, which has also been a system of livelihood for them. However, with the advances in technology, there has been an inevitable hike in reducing human resources. Choosing to create betterment for the world and humans by degrading the value of a human is questionable.*

10. *In the end, it all boils down to the fact that machines are capable of doing intense physical and calculative, repetitive work that multiple humans together may find confusing and cumbersome. However, no device is still capable of thinking or creating extraordinary innovations made by a single individual. It is essential to maintain segregation and a fruitful balance between AI and humans.*

CHAPTER 13

Overview

With the rise of artificial intelligence (AI), predominant questions arise on the coexistence of human intelligence and AI. Whether it is a competition or a collaboration? This chapter focuses on conceptualizing the answers for the same with the best available information and examples in the present time. The rise of this technology is aimed to decrease the amount of time and effort exerted on mundane tasks that can easily be taken up by a machine. So, now people are equipped with more time to focus on thinking, developing creative and innovative solutions and actions beyond the reach of AI.

A parallel is drawn to the fact that this allows humans to expend more energy on quality and strategic tasks, facilitating us to be more human. It also acknowledges that the natural tendency of humans to be flawed also implies that their creations are imperatively imperfect. When it comes to branding and marketing, though AI has widened its scope and perspectives through personalized services, it still requires human creativity and qualities to take it forward. The chapter further discusses how scientific research must focus on developing AI applications that could integrate with human intelligence to enhance productivity within the broad constraints of privacy and judgments.

AI Versus Humans

Change might be constant, but how much does that affect us? Accepting change is of utmost significance in this age and day when the world is taken by storm with marvels of technology and the miraculous creations of the human brain that manifest itself in every field, whether arts, science, literature. And, the more our curiosity for the unknown is satiated, the more the challenge is to cope with an upgraded environment where everything is made convenient to the point that human efforts and talent face the innate threat of being obsolete and a thing of the past.

The same concern that the great comedian and actor and above all, the genius, Charlie Chaplin, depicted through his masterpiece, *Hard Times*. When machines dominate humans, throwing them out of the picture, they created them in the first place. The scenario is daunting, and, probably 10 years before, it might have felt like a mere possible scenario that may or may not happen. However, the plight is different now. Progress is on its way to conquer the zenith of excellence, and we are left with the omnipresent debate of human intelligence versus AI. Will AI take over the realm of humans rendering human efforts futile and obsolete? Is the promising field of machine learning a wolf in the disguise of a lamb waiting to tear us down?

AI versus human intelligence—is it a competition or a collaboration?

According to Forrester, "Every industry will be dramatically disrupted by artificial intelligence (A.I.) applications very soon if they haven.t already been. In 2020, businesses that use A.I. to uncover new insights will take $1.2 trillion each year from competitors that don't."

AI, no doubt, has a notable dominance in multiple tasks, mainly when it appears to be about monotonous judgments:

Execution speed: Although a doctor can perform a diagnosis in about 10 minutes, the AI can simultaneously execute a million.

Unbiased: AI involves none to less biased opinions on the decision-making manner.

Operation: AI does not require as many pauses in their task because of overload as humans.

Accuracy: Preciseness of the output increases.

Does this mean that a technology that is the human mind's brainchild will disrupt the creator with its supremacy?

However, there is still a catch to it. Because no matter what, it is not easy for the creation to overtake its creator. Because there is a human filter that all the human hand products go through, the traces of which imperatively require the human touch are flawed and imperfect. Sometimes, imperfection even adds to the advantage.

As discussed in the previous chapter, the innate flaws always ensure a better space for improvement and innovation because of the human potential to change and adapt to the changing surroundings and needs.

Also, individual qualities and skills come with the patented trademark, *Human*. The qualities that cannot be mastered by machines. Machines can be organized and perfect and work with high-efficiency levels; however, the realm of creativity and innovation will always be dominated by humans, no matter how much machine learning progresses. Because mimicking will never equal what is real and raw. And, natural and raw are what help to strike a chord. It is similar to what Plato told about poetry being thrice removed from the truth. And, in this case, human creativity trumps the machine's perfection. To put it into a better set of words helps to strike a balance between them. A certain level of harmony lets both go hand in hand without disrupting or exploiting the other.

The rise of artificial intelligence is raising the premium on tasks that only humans can do: it is freeing workers from drudgery and allowing them to spend time on more strategic and valuable business activities. Instead of forcing people to spend time and effort on tasks that we find hard but computers find easy, we will be rewarded for doing what humans do best — and artificial intelligence will help make us all more human.

—Timo Elliott, Innovation Evangelist, SAP

What Is the Difference?

Nature

Human intelligence is all about adjusting to the environment using a mixture of several cognitive processes. Simultaneously, the AI platform is focused on designing machines that can mimic human behavior.

Memory

People use content consciousness and thinking whereas, AI is applying built-in instructions produced by specialists.

Learning

Human intelligence learns and reacts to the irregularities they encounter in life and the reactions or interactions, resulting in millions of functions overall in their lives. However, AI is limited or developed for particular jobs only, and its applicability on other tasks may not be readily attainable.

Having AI will be a boon to humanity. AI may enable us to solve global climate change. It can also lead to a rise in the pace of economic growth and level of production. **Let us have a look at the impact of AI in our world:**

1. AI's most evident impact is the rise of automation across a wide range of sectors, transforming it from manual to digital—more efficiently. Jobs that required repetition, data consumption, or vast data interpretation and management are now achieved by an AI—making it quicker and cost-effective.

2. As AI and machine learning execute, humans perform manual tasks, welcome new opportunities, build new industries, and innovative approaches to life and business. For example, digital engineering is an upcoming profession that came into the picture from the fast development of technology. So, although manual tasks may be gone, new jobs and occupations will be emerging along with the AI.

3. AI can unlock tons of businesses opportunities and improve productivity and participation within the organization. This, in turn, can increase demand for products and services and drive an economic growth model that delivers and enhances the quality of living.

4. As AI takes away some of the mundane tasks out of our hands, people now have more time to focus on thinking, developing creative and innovative solutions, and actions beyond the reach of AI and are squarely in the domain of human intelligence.

There is always the question of exploration versus exploitation when we talk about AI versus human. Exploring involves discovering newer realms of knowledge, looking into the unknown, and then using the tool of creativity to form better definitions. On the other hand, exploration is a complete refinement of the available resources, drawing out the last bit of what is available to make the best use. It is hard to say whether exploitation or exploration is the ideal way to harness the resources. Depending on the circumstances, we must balance both exploitations for creative optimization of resources and exploration for innovative ideas. The former is done best by AI, and the latter is done by humans, again underscoring the importance of a necessary balance, which is the ideal framework for both.

They are coming to the debate about AI versus human intelligence; recent AI progress mimics human intelligence even more closely now. However, machines still have a long way to match what human brains are capable of doing. Our ability to process and implement the *knowledge* we acquire, with a sense of *logic, reasoning, and experience*, makes us unique. While machines can mimic human behavior to some extent, their expertise to make a rational decision may fall behind in comparison to us. AI-powered machines lack "common sense" and are heavily dependent on information and events. AI systems are clueless in understanding **"action" and "consequences,"** hence cannot understand or operate on the **holistic human approach**. "With *knowledge* comes *power*, and with power comes great *responsibility*."

AI has made our tasks easier in some ways. But, it is far away from being perfect. There have been some significant *failures* that have raised questions about AI being a part of our lives:

1. While under computer control, Uber self-driving autonomous car killed a pedestrian.
2. Innocent people were incorrectly classified as possible criminals as AI-enabled facial recognition tools became biased toward colored skin tones.
3. IBM's Watson AI advised unsafe and inaccurate cancer treatments.
4. In short, it is not AI versus human that works, but AI and human, clubbed together, working in tune with each other, thereby drawing the best and most fruitful results. Through proper collaboration and strategy, both can work to enhance each other's strengths.

Even when it comes to branding and marketing, though AI has widened its scope and perspectives through personalized services, it still requires human creativity and qualities to take it forward. Because specific attributes like hard work, passion, determination, etc. cannot be comprehended by machines, machines can always sharpen those qualities, thereby leading to efficiency.

Humans + A.I.

The right perspective would be to AI's positive attributes with human intelligence to explain the significant gap separating human intelligence and AI. Scientific research should focus on developing AI applications that could integrate with human intelligence to enhance productivity within the broad constraints of privacy and judgments. If we will build a collaborative environment for both, it would surely open up new opportunities for many in numerous different fields.

Key Takeaways

1. *According to Forrester, "Every industry will be dramatically disrupted by artificial intelligence (A.I.) applications very soon if they haven.t already been. In 2020, businesses that use A.I. to uncover new insights will take $1.2 trillion each year from competitors that don't."*

2. *AI provides execution speed, nonbiased results, efficient operation, and accuracy.*

3. *Individual qualities and skills come with the patented trademark, Human. The qualities that cannot be mastered by machines. Machines can be organized and perfect and work with high-efficiency levels; however, the realm of creativity and innovation will always be dominated by humans.*

4. *Human intelligence is all about adjusting to the environment using a mixture of several cognitive processes. Simultaneously, the AI platform is focused on designing machines that can mimic human behavior.*

5. *People use content consciousness and thinking, whereas AI is applying built-in instructions produced by specialists.*

6. *As AI and machine learning execute, humans perform manual tasks, welcome new opportunities, build new industries, and innovative approaches to life and business.*

7. *AI-powered machines lack "common sense" and are heavily dependent on information and events. AI systems are clueless in understanding "action" and "consequences," hence cannot understand or operate on the holistic human approach. "With knowledge comes power, and with power comes great responsibility."*

8. *AI has made our tasks easier in some ways. But, it is far away from being perfect. There have been some significant failures that have raised questions about AI being a part of our lives.*

9. *The right perspective would be to AI's positive attributes with human intelligence to explain the significant gap separating human intelligence and AI.*

CHAPTER 14

Future of AI

Overview

The various concepts and case studies discussed in the preceding chapters exemplify the multitude of ways artificial intelligence (AI) is changing the face of marketing and business. AI Researcher Eliezer Yudkowsky states that anything with the capability to compete and contribute at the same level as human intelligence is surely bound to add value to the betterment of the world. This chapter focuses on exploring the future of AI, which encourages businesses and investors globally to participate in reaping benefits from it. Although it is still at a nascent stage where it is far from being tagged as "transformational" or "revolutionary," individual AI-powered systems are expected to improve their performance based on the data they analyze. This improvement will be incredibly advantageous in reducing the uncertainties concerning the future of this technology. AI has the potential to transform the traditional methods of marketing, sales, and customer services through cost reduction, risk management, growth acceleration, and opportunities. Companies can use AI tools to build customized experiences based on information extracted from factors like human emotions and data is further explored. AI runs parallel to humans because every human's merit point is their ability to learn, adapt, and change according to the ever-evolving demands and on the rise. While the standing evidence of AI's innovative future through easing the path of success could, however, inherently risk the human workforce. In the case of an evolving and promising technology like AI, with viable skill manifestations in the present, the future holds an ocean load of possibilities.

The future is an unknown realm, filled with uncertainties and vague ideas, in short, a hazy maze. However, that does not stop us, humans, from peeking into that maze and trying our best to draw out a hypothetical picture of a probable future. From time immemorial, the question mark that is the future characteristic is what humans are most eager to solve. Everything we do, everything we create is with this innate knowledge or awareness about a probable future, as uncertain as it is. One of the most essential and crucial qualities a business person must possess is prudence, the ability to look into the future and take necessary actions.

AI is a promising field with an ocean depth of potential that can make a world of difference when utilized correctly. The previous chapters and the various case studies we went through can attest to the multitude of ways AI is changing the face of marketing and business. For someone visiting us from the past, AI's fantastic potential and scope is enough to blow their minds.

According to AI Researcher Eliezer Yudkowsky,

Anything that could give rise to smarter than human intelligence, brain-computer interfaces, or neuroscience-based human intelligence enhancement – wins hands down beyond contest as doing the most to change the world. Nothing else is even in the same league.

AI has already made its voice heard as a technology that can be transformational and revolutionary, though that journey still has a long road to traverse. However, the futuristic nature of AI does not stop businesses and investors all over the world from attesting to its prowess and brilliance, transforming the whole face of marketing, sales, and customer services through cost reduction, risk management, growth acceleration, and through its innovative approach, enhancing possibilities and opportunities.

The enormous magnitude of growth in revenue and profits that AI can achieve through its different marketing, sales, and customer services approach. Almost adding a redefined stature to each blends AI's prospects with the colors of brilliance and unquestionable genius that has fantastic potential to reform and redefine.

Let's take a closer look at the impact of AI in each of these fields, namely:

- Sales
- Marketing
- Customer service

Sales

When it comes to sales, algorithms is the word to be added. The filter added by AI refines the field to its reachable potential. An algorithm is "a finite sequence of well defined, computer-implementable instructions, typically to solve a class of problems or to perform a computation." Algorithms are used generally for calculations, data processing, and automated reasoning.

Sales organizations are reaping spellbinding profits by utilizing and proper execution of these algorithms, which help narrow down their targets, which in turn helps inefficient utilization of available resources and high yields with minimal costs.

Algorithms help with the accounting bases, leading and indicating the paths that will lead to success quicker than the rest. In other words, it helps in prioritization, pointing out the sales that would lead to profits and identifying areas where the deployment of resources can create the most impact.

Marketing

AI-powered marketing solutions add new dimensions to the field, enhancing results through their customer-specific and target-oriented strategies. Some of the famous names that use AI in their backdrop are Netflix, Amazon, and unquestionably, Google. And, the widespread and immense popularity of this platform and the effectiveness with which they deliver their services, ensuring customer satisfaction, can attest to AI's promising potential and can be harnessed to reap tremendous results.

AI-enhanced advertising, highly personalized website experience, AI-directed content creation, chatbots, and so on are examples of services that sharpen and polish the field upon which they act.

Customer Services

Any business's ultimate aim is maximum profits with minimum cost while ensuring a fixed position in the market, which is adaptable enough to be upgraded and developed concerning the changing environment and market demands. And, an effective means to this end is customer satisfaction, which ensures the goals aforementioned. A satisfied customer is a standing proof for its efficiency and a channel for its development and progress.

The more the customer experience is enhanced, there are higher chances for customer satisfaction. As is evident, the best way to make a customer feel at home with a brand is through providing them exclusively curated services that match their interests and preferences. And, AI achieves this through a variety of channels like automation, sentiment analysis, natural language processing (NLP), and so on.

It is a widely known and accepted phrase that "Rome wasn't built in a day." The same goes for any endeavor that has reaped results, and that will reap results. Though AI's potential and its ability to change and innovate cannot be denied, the fact stands that the effects of AI are not yet in the realm, which can be called **"Transformational" or "revolutionary."** Those two are still hypothetical terms that aren't however utterly unachievable in the near future with the right use of the right strategies. Because more often than not, the results of AI work directly proportional to how they are handled and managed by the managers and people concerned. In short, the future of AI, to a large extent, is determined by how it is polished and sharpened in the present.

While talking about the present, it is essential to look at the standing evidence of AI's intelligent effects that ensure an innovative future, which can include an underlying challenge for the human skill and workforce, thereby opening another channel of the persistent debate of human versus AI and its unavoidable manifestations in the future. Let us take a closer look at these implications by analyzing the present implementations of AI that are currently in progress.

Writing in Newer Techniques or Writing Away Writers Off the Book?

Content creation is a crucial element in digital marketing. It is the magnet that attracts the target audience, thereby channeling the business's growth and development. Therefore, it is imperative that content writers work with precision and sharpness, creating content that hits home and makes the desired effect. It should not be superficial or ambiguous; rather, clarity must be its defining point blended with the right amount of creativity.

There are a lot of AI-powered tools that back up content creation, increasing their impact and reach. These innovative tools help to do away with the manual and somewhat repetitive conventional techniques that can be draining and strenuous and, at times, not efficient enough when compared to the hours of work put in. Therefore, the emergence of automation and AI-driven content marketing platforms are proving to be extremely beneficial for businesses.

When it comes to digital marketing, keywords are the key. This fact is proved by the level of importance placed on search engine optimization (SEO) and the corresponding tools. However, it is as strenuous as it is essential because keyword research is not always a piece of cake, and it can be extremely draining and time-consuming. Both these elements, that is, time and energy, are not something we have in plenty in this time and day. And, investing a large amount of that on manual keyword search while running around the clock can prove to be touching the realms of futility and wastage.

And, that is why, businesses have shifted their focus to automated keyword search powered by AI, thereby saving both time and energy and, by default, the cost, and resources.

Some examples of AI-powered SEO tools are, Twinword, Keyword Country, LSI Graph, and so on, all of which help speed up the search process.

Content writing is as important as SEO, and it is a term that is highly regarded as a human forte. Content creation requires fresh ideas, an innovative approach, a very in-depth understanding of the subject matter and the audience, and the precision and skill to bring all these under the umbrella of creativity. These highly human aspects might seem impossible for technology to adapt. However, it might come as a surprise that many AI-powered content creation platforms enhance the content, easing the paths to success, with the inherent risk to the human workforce in the future.

Some examples of this are Wordsmith, Quill, WordAI, Articoolo, and so on.

Redesigning the Future of Design

At present, in design, the effects and impacts of AI are limited to providing the color palette based on the mood and personality. However, this does not mean that there is no space for future progress. In the case of an evolving and promising technology like AI, with viable skill manifestations in the present, the future holds an ocean load of possibilities. With possibilities that can be explored and built upon. Similar stories from the past throw light on various technologies whose brilliance and power to change were revealed gradually, like the Internet.

In the future, companies can use AI tools to build a complete visual identity based on the brand personality map based on factors such as human emotions and data.

Marketing Campaigns

When it comes to marketing, adhering to the customer's needs is of utmost importance, for if the customer is happy, the brand receives fuel for growth and development. And, over time, more focus has been placed on the customer as an individual rather than the usual generalized approach of conventional marketing strategies.

However, with the advent of AI, it is possible to provide personalized and exclusive services to the target customers ensuring maximum satisfaction and customer loyalty. At present, AI-powered tools can discern the right time for presenting a particular advertisement to the audience to get full engagement.

And, the future holds a greater possibility to customize the advertisements for every target audience using emotional manipulation.

Stating AI abilities does not mean that we belittle the human capacity or rather the human touch. However, the fact still stands that AI has a more extraordinary ability to apply its prowess over a larger scale and analyze data, thereby determining what works and what does not. This ability is of great significance to advertising since advertising costs a good deal of money, and it cannot afford the loss of not reaping an immediate return. Therefore, they need to work with precision and sharpness to strike when the iron is still hot, and this is what AI helps them achieve.

Another gem is added to the crown of AI because it can identify potential customers for the business, which is as good as finding newer grounds to grow and develop, which ultimately is the aim of any ambitious company.

And, one cannot deny that AI is eventually taking over the world of advertising by storm, opening new doors and offering better dimensions and perspectives. Because AI is doing way more than just creating ads with human involvement, it is transforming and upgrading the world of advertising in every way possible.

All these are only the take-off points of AI. A technology that can impact this extension would have a lot in store that can be revealed through real innovation and upgrading. Adding to this is those specific AI systems can learn and develop either with humans' help or on their own, which takes their potential to the next level of brilliance. Because here, AI runs parallel to humans because every human's merit point is their ability to learn, adapt, and change according to the ever-evolving demands and on the rise.

Individual AI-powered systems to improve their performance based on the data they analyze strengthens this point, adding firmer foundations and reducing the uncertainties concerning the future of AI.

Key Takeaways

1. *Anything that could give rise to smarter than human intelligence, brain–computer interfaces, or neuroscience-based human intelligence enhancement wins hands down beyond contest as doing the most to change the world. Nothing else is even in the same league.*

2. *The enormous magnitude of growth in revenue and profits that AI can achieve through its different marketing, sales, and customer services approach. Almost adding a redefined stature to each blends AI's prospects with the colors of brilliance and unquestionable genius that has fantastic potential to reform and redefine.*

3. *Sales organizations are reaping spellbinding profits by utilizing and proper execution of AI, which helps narrow down their targets, which in turn helps inefficient utilization of available resources and high yields with minimal costs.*

4. *The more the customer experience is enhanced, there are higher chances for customer satisfaction. As is evident, the best way to make a customer feel at home with a brand is through providing them exclusively curated services that match their interests and preferences. And, AI achieves this through a variety of channels like automation, sentiment analysis, natural language processing (NLP), and so on.*

5. *AI-enhanced advertising, highly personalized website experience, AI-directed content creation, chatbots, and so on are examples of services that sharpen and polish the field upon which they act.*

6. *There are a lot of AI-powered tools that back up content creation, increasing their impact and reach. These innovative tools help to do away with the manual and somewhat repetitive conventional techniques that can be draining and strenuous and, at times, not efficient enough when compared to the hours of work put in.*

7. *Companies may use AI tools to build a complete visual identity based on the brand personality map based on factors such as human emotions and data.*

8. *With the advent of AI, it is possible to provide personalized and exclusive services to the target customers ensuring maximum satisfaction and customer loyalty. At present, AI-powered tools can discern the right time for presenting a particular advertisement to the audience to get full engagement.*

Resources and Workbook

List of Brand Tone of Voice

Tone Word	Meaning
Abashed	Ashamed or embarrassed; also, disconcerted
Absurd	Ridiculous; silly.
Accusatory	A tone of accusation; to accuse of a crime or offense
Admonishing	Cautioning, reproving or scolding; especially in a mild and good-willed manner; reminding
Adoring	To regard with esteem, love, and respect; honor
Amused	Pleasurably entertained, occupied, or diverted
Apathetic	Having or showing little or no emotion; indifferent or unresponsive
Benevolent	Characterized by or expressing goodwill or kindly feelings
Bewildered	Completely puzzled or confused; perplexed
Biting	Sarcastic, having a biting or sarcastic tone
Bitter	Characterized by intense antagonism or hostility
Blunt	Abrupt in manner; obtuse
Bold	Not hesitating or fearful in the face of danger or rebuff; courageous and daring
Brusque	Abrupt in manner; blunt; rough
Calm	Free from excitement or passion; tranquil
Candid	Frank; outspoken
Cheery	In good spirits
Churlish	Critical or harsh in a mean-spirited way
Comic	Funny; humorous
Commanding	Imposing; having an air of superiority
Conceited	Having an excessively favorable opinion of one's self or abilities
Contentious	Argumentative, quarrelsome
Curt	Rudely brief in speech or abrupt
Desperate	Having an urgent need, desire

Tone Word	Meaning
Detached	Impartial or objective; disinterested; unbiased/ not concerned; aloof
Diabolic	Devilish; fiendish; outrageously wicked
Disbelieving	To have no belief in; refuse or reject belief in
Disdainful	Expressing contempt or disdain
Disgusted	To excite nausea or loathing in To offend the taste or moral sense of
Disrespectful	Showing a lack of respect; rude and discourteous
Disturbed	Marked by symptoms of mental illness
Doubtful	Uncertain outcome or result
Dramatic	Of or pertaining to drama; excessively confrontational
Dreary	Causing sadness or gloom
Earnest	Serious in intention or sincerely zealous
Ebullient	Overflowing with enthusiasm, or excitement; high-spirited
Ecstatic	In a state of ecstasy; rapturous
Effusive	Unreserved or unduly demonstrative
Egotistical	Vain; boastful; indifferent to the well-being of others; selfish
Elated	Very happy or proud; jubilant; in high spirits
Embarrassed	To feel self-conscious or ill at ease
Enraged	To make extremely angry; put into a rage; infuriate
Enthusiastic	Excited; energetic
Evasive	Ambiguous; cryptic; unclear
Excited	Emotionally aroused; stirred
Facetious	Inappropriate; flippant
Flippant	Superficial; glib; shallow; thoughtless; frivolous
Forceful	Powerful; energetic; confident; assertive
Formal	Respectful; stilted; factual; following accepted styles/rules
Frank	Honest; direct; plain; matter-of-fact
Frustrated	Annoyed; discouraged
Gentle	Kind; considerate; mild; soft
Ghoulish	Delighting in the revolting or the loathsome
Grim	Serious; gloomy; depressing; lacking humor; macabre
Gullible	Naïve; innocent; ignorant
Hard	Unfeeling; hard-hearted; unyielding
Humble	Deferential; modest
Humorous	Amusing; entertaining; playful

Tone Word	Meaning
Hypercritical	Unreasonably critical; hair splitting; nitpicking
Impartial	Unbiased; neutral; objective
Impassioned	Filled with emotion; ardent
Imploring	Pleading; begging
Impressionable	Trusting; child-like
Inane	Silly; foolish; stupid; nonsensical
Incensed	Enraged
Incredulous	Disbelieving; unconvinced; questioning; suspicious
Indignant	Annoyed; angry; dissatisfied
Informative	Instructive; factual; educational
Inspirational	Encouraging; reassuring
Intense	Earnest; passionate; concentrated; deeply felt
Intimate	Familiar; informal; confidential; confessional
Ironic	The opposite of what is meant
Irreverent	Lacking respect for things that are generally taken seriously
Jaded	Bored; having had too much of the same thing; lack enthusiasm
Joyful	Positive; optimistic; cheerful; elated
Judgmental	Critical; finding fault; disparaging
Light-Hearted	Carefree; relaxed; chatty; humorous
Loving	Affectionate; showing intense, deep concern
Macabre	Gruesome; horrifying; frightening
Malicious	Desiring to harm others or to see others suffer; ill-willed; spiteful
Mean-Spirited	Inconsiderate; unsympathetic
Mocking	Scornful; ridiculing; making fun of someone
Mourning	Grieving; lamenting; woeful
Naïve	Innocent; unsophisticated; immature
Narcissistic	Self-admiring; selfish; boastful; self-pitying
Nasty	Unpleasant; unkind; disagreeable; abusive
Negative	Unhappy, pessimistic
Nostalgic	Thinking about the past; wishing for something from the past
Objective	Without prejudice; without discrimination; fair; based on fact
Optimistic	Hopeful; cheerful
Outraged	Angered and resentful; furious; extremely angered
Outspoken	Frank; candid; spoken without reserve
Pathetic	Expressing pity, sympathy, tenderness

Tone Word	Meaning
Patronizing	Condescending; scornful; pompous
Pensive	Reflective; introspective; philosophical; contemplative
Persuasive	Convincing; eloquent; influential; plausible
Pessimistic	Seeing the negative side of things
Philosophical	Theoretical; analytical; rational; logical
Playful	Full of fun and good spirits; humorous; jesting
Pragmatic	Realistic; sensible
Pretentious	Affected; artificial; grandiose; rhetorical; flashy
Regretful	Apologetic; remorseful
Resentful	Aggrieved; offended; displeased; bitter
Resigned	Accepting; unhappy
Restrained	Controlled; quiet; unemotional
Reverent	showing deep respect and esteem
Righteous	Morally right and just; guiltless; pious; god-fearing
Scathing	Critical; stinging; unsparing; harsh
Scornful	Expressing contempt or derision; scathing; dismissive
Sentimental	Thinking about feelings, especially when remembering the past
Sincere	Honest; truthful; earnest
Solemn	Not funny; in earnest; serious
Thoughtful	Reflective; serious; absorbed
Tolerant	Open-minded; charitable; patient; sympathetic; lenient
Tragic	Disastrous; calamitous
Unassuming	Modest; self-effacing; restrained
Uneasy	Worried; uncomfortable; edgy; nervous
Virtuous	Lawful; righteous; moral; upstanding
Whimsical	Quaint; playful; mischievous; offbeat
Witty	Clever; quick-witted; entertaining
Wonder	Awe-struck; admiring; fascinating
Worried	Anxious; stressed; fearful

List of Brand Values

A
Abundance, Acceptance, Accessibility, Accountability, Accuracy, Activeness, Adaptability, Adventure, Affection, Ambition, Appreciation, Approachability, Attention to detail

B, C
Balance, Beauty, Belonging, Bravery, Capability, Care, Change, Charity, Clarity, Cleanliness, Collaboration, Comfort, Commitment, Communication, Compassion, Confidence, Connection, Consistency, Control, Cooperation, Courage, Craftiness, Craftsmanship, Creativity, Credibility, Curiosity, Customer satisfaction, Customer-centric

D, E
Daring, Dedication, Dependability, Determination, Devotion, Dignity, Diligence, Directness, Discipline, Discovery, Discretion, Diversity, Dreams, Drive, Duty, Eagerness, Ease of use, Economy, Education, Effectiveness, Elegance, Empathy, Empowering, Energy, Engagement, Enjoyment, Entertainment, Enthusiasm, Entrepreneurship, Environment, Equality, Evolution, Excellence, Excitement, Exhilaration, Expertise, Exploration

F, G
Fairness, Faith, Family, Fame, Fascination, Fearlessness, Firmness, Fitness, Flexibility, Focus, Freedom, Freshness, Friendship, Fun, Generosity, Genius, Genuineness, Goodwill, Gratitude, Growth, Guidance

H, I
Happiness, Hard work, Harmony, Health, Heart, Heroism, History, Honesty, Honor, Hope, Humility, Humor, Imagination, Impact, Individuality, Innovation, Insight, Inspiration, Integrity, Intelligence, Intimacy, Intuition

J, K, L

Joy, Justice, Kindness, Knowledge, Leadership, Learning, Liveliness, Logic, Longevity, Love, Loyalty

M, N, O

Mastery, Mindfulness, Motivation, Neatness, Optimism, Organization, Originality

P, Q

Partnership, Passion, Patience, Peace, Perception, Performance, Persistence, Personal development, Playfulness, Poise, Polish, Popularity, Positivity, Potential, Power, Precision, Pride, Privacy, Productivity, Professionalism, Progress, Purity, Quality

R, S

Recognition, Reflection, Relationships, Reliability, Resilience, Resourcefulness, Respect, Responsibility, Safety, Satisfaction, Security, Sharing, Simplicity, Sincerity, Skill, Speed, Spontaneity, Stability, Strength, Success, Support, Sustainability

T, U, V, W

Talent, Teamwork, Thoughtfulness, Tolerance, Trust, Truth, Understanding, Uniqueness, Unity, Value, Variety, Virtue, Vision, Warmth, Welcoming, Wonder

List of Brand Personality

The Lover—Chanel, Magnum, Dior, BMW, Victoria Secret
(Famous industries: fragrance, cosmetics, wine, indulgent food, indulgent travel)

The Explorer—Jeep, Red Bull, The North Face
(Famous industries: extreme sports, outdoor equipment, automotive (SUV category), adventure travel)

The Sage—Google, Audi, IBM, BBC
(Famous industries: media and news networks, schools and universities, educational businesses, consultancies, search engines)

The Jester—Nando's, M&Ms, Dollar Shave Club
(Famous industries: confectionary, professional services, beer/lager, child services)

The Ruler—Louis Vuitton, Rolex, Mercedes-Benz
(Famous industries: automotive (luxury), watch manufacturers, hotels, formal wear apparel, any brands providing luxury or high quality)

The Magician—Disney, Dyson, Coca-Cola
(Famous industries: health, beauty, entertainment, relaxation, well-being)

The Caregiver—UNICEF, WWF, TOMS
(Famous industries: health and aged care, not-for-profits, hospitals, education)

The Innocent—Dove, Aveeno, Innocent
(Famous industries: beauty and skin products, organic, cleaning, fresh food, anything you put in or on the body)

The Everyman—IKEA, Target, LYNX, Gap
(Famous industries: me/family life, comfort foods, everyday apparel, automobile (family/everyday))

The Hero—Nike, Land Rover, Adidas, FedEx
(Famous industries: sportswear, sports equipment, outdoor/tactical equipment, emergency, trade services (plumbing, electricity, locksmiths, mechanic))

The Creator—Lego, Adobe, Apple
(Famous industries: arts, design, information technology, marketing, writing)
The Outlaw—Virgin, Harley–Davidson, Diesel
(Famous industries: automobile (motorcycles), destruction tools, alternative apparel, body art)

Core Dimensions of Personality Traits

Sincerity: down-to-earth, honest, wholesome, cheerful
(Disney, Hallmark, Amazon, Cadbury)
Excitement: daring, spirited, imaginative, up-to-date
(Tesla, Red Bull, Coca-Cola, Nike)
Competence: reliable, intelligent, successful
(Volvo, Google, Intel, Microsoft)
Sophistication: upper class, charming
(Tiffany, Rolex, Gucci, Apple)
Ruggedness: outdoorsy, tough
(Harley–Davidson, Timberland, Jeep, Marlboro)
Identify the desire that you want your brand to evoke and use that to build the personality.

Workbook

Purpose of your Brand

Why do you exist?

_____

How are you different?

_____

What problem are you solving?

_____

Competitor Research

Message			
Visual			
Quality of offering			
Review/feedback			
Marketing channels			
Best campaign			
Worst campaign			

Target Demographics

AGE :

LOCATION :

GENDER :

INCOME :

EDUCATION :

MARITAL OR FAMILY STATUS :

OCCUPATION :

ETHNIC BACKGROUND :

PERSONALITY :

ATTITUDES :

VALUES :

INTERESTS :

What value does your product or service provide to your customer's life?

_____

How and when will your customer use the product or service?

_____

What features are attractive to your customer?

_____

Branding AI tool evaluation

DIGITAL TOOL	OBJECTIVE	CUSTOMERS	COMPETITORS	EASE OF USE
Which tool are you considering?	Which strategic objective does it facilitate?	What your customer uses and potential impact could it have on them?	Do your competitors use this tool? Does it appear to be effective?	How easy would it be to use this tool?
E.g., Hootsuite	E.g., Increase sales by 40%.	Customers use ABC to share lifestyle photos and engage with influencers.	Competitors use XYZ to advertise discounts and promotions, but customers do not respond.	Training required for staff with lower confidence.

References

Andreassen, T.W., and L.L. Olsen. 2008. *The Impact of Customers' Perception of Varying Degrees of Customer Service on Commitment and Perceived Relative Attractiveness.* Norwegian School of Management, Oslo, Norway; Emerald Group Publishing Limited. https://ukessays.com/essays/marketing/theories-and-relevant-models-about-branding-marketing-essay.php#citethis

De Chernatony, L., and F. Dall'Olmo Riley. 1998. "Defining a "brand": Beyond the Literature with Experts' Interpretations." *Journal of Marketing Management* 14, no. 5, 417–443. http://doi.org//10.1362/026725798784867798

UKEssays. November 2018. "Theories and Relevant Models about Branding." Retrieved from https://ukessays.com/essays/marketing/theories-and-relevant-models-about-branding-marketing-essay.php?vref=1

UKEssays. November 2018. "Brand Perception and Customer Buying Behaviour." Retrieved from https://ukessays.com/essays/marketing/brand-perception-and-customer-buying-behaviour-marketing-essay.php?vref=1

About the Author

Chahat Aggarwal is the Founder and CEO of Impact Study Biz. Impact Study Biz leverages artificial intelligence (AI) and data science to generate brand strategies. She helps organizations build and grow their business through leading expert and research-backed strategies, which help them unlock their true potential. According to Chahat, "Perseverance is the path for accomplishing joy and success." Her positivity and "can-do attitude" help her tread to some of the most complex projects and endeavors.

Chahat Aggarwal, an award-winning entrepreneur, is a figure of authority in the realm of all things branding and digital. Having lived in multiple countries, she has a keen understanding of global consumer psychology. A prolific brand strategist helps organizations tap into their latent brand potential. She has helped over 20 global brands and established them in over 45 countries. When not drawing strategies for clients, Chahat is busy advocating gender equality as a UN women member and helps educate about mental health via authorship for Thrive Global, USA.

Her experience teamed with understanding with a firm foundation on fair market and equal opportunities paves the way for a work culture that is a blend of uniqueness and determination to achieve more. She is featured among top 10 women entrepreneurs in India by FORBES, she has won India Achievers Award, won most promising women entrepreneur of 2020, and many more.

As soon as she completed her online Strategic Negotiation Certification from Yale University, she got the opportunity to become part of India's biggest hospitality startup—"OYO." Within a time span of two years, she played a crucial role in the brand's valuation from $250 million to $10 billion. By deeply understanding and balancing the need of customers and the services offered by the brand, she sets a realistic approach, which helps in governing the desired results. She has the ability to successfully acknowledge and optimize brands in terms of creating and generating revenue. She believes and helps brands turn their business into money-making assets. She bases her strategic plans on in-depth research to ensure the best impact-driven results for every brand, no matter the industry, product, or service.

Index

Letter 'f' and 't' after locators indicate figure and table, respectively.

OTHER TITLES IN THE MARKETING COLLECTION

Naresh Malhotra, Georgia Tech, Editor

- *The Business Design Cube* by Rajagopal
- *Customer Relationship Management* by Michael Pearce
- *Stand Out!* by Brian McGurk
- *The Coming Age of Robots* by George Pettinico and George R. Milne
- *Market Entropy* by Rajagopal
- *Decoding Customer Value at the Bottom of the Pyramid* by Ritu Srivastava
- *Qualitative Marketing Research* by Rajagopal
- *Social Media Marketing* by Alan Charlesworth
- *Employee Ambassadorship* by Michael W. Lowenstein
- *Service Excellence* by Ruth N. Bolton
- *Critical Thinking for Marketers, Volume I* by David Dwight, David Soorholtz, and Terry Grapentine
- *Critical Thinking for Marketers, Volume II* by David Dwight, David Soorholtz, and Terry Grapentine
- *Relationship Marketing Re-Imagined* by Naresh Malhotra, Can Uslay, and Ahmet Bayraktar
- *Marketing Plan Templates for Enhancing Profits* by Elizabeth Rush Kruger

Announcing the Business Expert Press Digital Library

Concise e-books business students need for classroom and research

This book can also be purchased in an e-book collection by your library as

- a one-time purchase,
- that is owned forever,
- allows for simultaneous readers,
- has no restrictions on printing, and
- can be downloaded as PDFs from within the library community.

Our digital library collections are a great solution to beat the rising cost of textbooks. E-books can be loaded into their course management systems or onto students' e-book readers.
The **Business Expert Press** digital libraries are very affordable, with no obligation to buy in future years. For more information, please visit **www.businessexpertpress.com/librarians**. To set up a trial in the United States, please email **sales@businessexpertpress.com**.

www.ingramcontent.com/pod-product-compliance
Lightning Source LLC
Chambersburg PA
CBHW061208220326
41599CB00025B/4573